NOUVELLE COUCHSIDE

Turkey Toast Tubs

White bread
Ketchup, mustard with horseradish
Salt, pepper
Turkey meat hot dog
Squeeze Parkay

Stack three slices of bread and mold them into the shape of a satellite dish. Shred turkey frank with scissors and fill the dish. Garnish heavily with ketchup and mustard and pinch bread into pouch around it. Glaze with Squeeze Parkay and pop into oven until golden brown. Serve hot.

THE COUCH POTATO® GUIDE TO LIFE

Text by Jack Mingo

**Illustrations and additional text by
Robert Armstrong**

**Recipes and additional text by
Allan Dodge**

AVON
PUBLISHERS OF BARD, CAMELOT, DISCUS AND FLARE BOOKS

THE COUCH POTATO® GUIDE TO LIFE is an original publication of
Avon Books.

AVON BOOKS
A division of
The Hearst Corporation
105 Madison Avenue
New York, New York 10016

First Avon Books Mass Market Printing: March 1988
First Avon Books Trade Printing: July 1985

Video Personae

Jack Mingo's writing credits include *The Official Couch Potato Handbook* (Capra Press, 1983), *Dr. Davenport Spudd Talks to Couch Potato Teens, Dr. Spudd's Etiquette for the Couch Potato* and numerous articles. He lives in Oakland, California.

Robert Armstrong, Couch Potato Elder #2 and a founder of the Movement, provided the illustrations and text for the pictorial features and furnished additional ideas throughout the book. He co-edits *The Tuber's Voice*, the Couch Potato newsletter, and is the creator of comic book character Mickey Rat.

Allan "Chef Aldo" Dodge, Couch Potato Elder #3 and another founder of the Movement, contributed recipes and other text for the food/snack section and provided inspiration throughout the book.

Patricia Graves, co-editor and columnist for *The Tuber's Voice*, was responsible for the design, typography and layout.

Special Thanks To:

Brad Bunnin for his suggestions and advice, to whom we owe everything—or at least 10%.

Ken Taylor, Eeva MacFeeley, Madeline Leullier, Lena Zwalve, Ric Lawson, Guilia Centineo, Adam Woog, Kako Takahashi, Roger Mingo, Gloria McCracken, Tom Iacino, Maria Moeel and Nuna James for ideas and translations.

The thousands of Couch Potatoes across the world whose encouragement and example have kept us going.

Couchland, Couchland, Tuber Alles

Table of Contents

INTRODUCTION

A Few Notes About This Book

If you prefer to watch large quantities of Television and avoid books, this may be one of the most important pieces of reading matter you have ever taken your eyes from the screen for—even more crucial than the latest *TV Guide*. We don't suggest that you miss valuable viewing time to read it; instead, why not take it a short segment at a time during less-than-vital programming like the news, certain commercials, halftime shows, presidential speeches and PBS pledge breaks? In fact, this is exactly how the book was written—to make each subsection just the right length for reading while viewing.

Video Repression

Yet, for all these successes, TV viewers continue to be oppressed, ridiculed and devalued. Our favorite shows are subject to unpredictable and disturbing schedule changes, preemptions and even outright cancellations, resulting all too often in chronic anxiety and emotional trauma. The twin evils of TV Puritanism and Video Guilt are insurmountable barricades to pleasurable Prolonged Viewing for millions of videophiles . And basic necessities we consider the birthright of every American—satellite dishes, VCRs, cable-ready stereo projection TVs, full-service cable systems and a sufficient supply of gourmet snack food—are still out of financial reach for most of us.

So it's clear that there's plenty to accomplish before TV viewers get the kind of respect and gratitude we deserve for our contributions to present-day society. After all, we are consumers of the first order in an economy that depends on consumption. Our reflective, relaxed life-style is the perfect antidote to the high-pressure, motion-crazed modern norm. In our meditative, alpha-wave-enhanced viewing, we absorb the vicarious wisdom and experience of lifetimes, qualifying us for what should be an honored place in the world as repositories of the Great Truths of our culture.

Ultimately, then, this book was written as a guide to heavy viewers who wish to enhance the many intellectual, physical, psychological, societal, familial and interpersonal benefits of bountiful Television viewing; and as a warning to those who view insufficiently. Aside from your 25-inch Sony, La-Z-Boy, toaster oven, lifetime subscription to *TV Guide* and official Couch Potato membership card, this may be the most important object you have ever allowed into your viewing module. Read it with your Television on, your feet up and your mind open.

What Is a Couch Potato?

Couch Potatoes, as their name implies, are happiest when vegetating "all eyes" in front of Television, stretched out in an overstuffed piece of furniture. These Tubers grew underground for many years until the intellectual and social climate warmed enough for them to sprout into the world.

Couch Tomatoes are the women's offshoot within the organization (see page 65).

Other Terms You May Be Unfamiliar With

Viewmaster: A higher rank of Couch Potatoism achieved through logging thousands of viewing hours and exhibiting extraordinary familiarity with classic TV shows of past and present.

Televisionary: Having reached the highest point of Couch Potato mysticism, Televisionaries have transcended making value judgments on TV programming and are subsequently able to watch *anything*—even test patterns, "snow" and *Strawberry Shortcake and Friends*—and appreciate its cosmic significance. Only Televisionaries are eligible to become Couch Potato Elders, the group of nine that heads the organization.

Simulviewing: Watching three or more TV shows at the same time so you don't miss anything good, so you can live thousands of lifetimes of vicarious experience in each week of viewing and so you can learn to break out of conventional, linear thinking patterns. Many Couch Potatoes of the Televisionary rank regularly simulview eight or more TV screens with up to 95% comprehension.

Lodge: While there is much to be said for small-group and solitary viewing, many Tubers like to gather together in support groups of like-minded peers for megahours of viewing. In addition, lodges offer seminars in new viewing techniques, companionship, shared video equipment and erudite discussions (during commercials) of issues like The Sitcom: Dead, or Merely Sleeping? Ann Sothern: As Funny As Lucy? and Hopalong Cassidy: Determinist Deist or Existential Nihilist?

To join an existing lodge, or found your own, see page 109.

Lifelong Viewing

A Goal of Lifelong Viewing

Sixty-nine percent of all Americans are too young, thank Sarnoff, to remember the deprivation of life before Television. Based on current viewing patterns, the average American will spend a full *nine years* watching Television between the ages of 2 and 65.

Life is short. Nine years of Television is not enough for those of us who want life to be more than just average. We want more and better viewing for ourselves, our children, our parents, grandparents, spouses and friends. Besides the prime time of viewing (ages 20-65), there are critical stages of life that we want to pay special attention to. These are:

Tubal Pregnancy (prenatal viewing through infancy)
The VHF Years (2 to 13)
The Teen Years
Late Show (65+)
Sign Off (viewing posthumously)

Video in utero.

Tubal Pregnancy:
A Womb With a View

"A woman watched the *Tale of Two Cities* miniseries while she
was pregnant. When her kid was born he was full of the dickens."

—Modern vaudeville routine

It is a well-known fact that
the development of a fetus is
directly related to its mother's
diet, attitude and activities during
pregnancy. TV watching has long
been a favorite activity among
pregnant women, probably because they somehow intuit how
much it benefits them and their
child.

TV is relaxing—just what the
doctor ordered for jittery expectant parents. The healing blue and
red light rays from a color TV have
been shown to increase natural
hormonal activity, increase restful
alpha waves in the brain and
create a warm, relaxed feeling of
well-being.

What many expectant mothers
fail to realize, though, is that they
may unwittingly be molding the
characters, future career choices
and interests of their children
through their TV viewing.

Babies can hear in the womb
and sense their mothers' emotional reactions. When babies
hear the Television and sense
their mothers' progressive relax-
ation and euphoria, they are
imprinted. Later when they hear

similar sounds they subconsciously re-experience those good feel-
ings, even if the sounds occur
years, even decades, later. Through
a complicated set of still unex-
plained phenomena, the babies
will tend to emulate some or all of
that which their mothers viewed
on Television while pregnant.

The signs are everywhere. Do
you think it is a coincidence that
the "punk" style was most popular
among kids who prenatally
watched *The Munsters* and *The
Addams Family?* That a dispro-
portionate number of transves-
tites were born in the years Milton
Berle was wearing women's
clothes on the *Texaco Star
Theatre?* That the mothers who
watched *Mr. Wizard* bore the
current crop of technicians and
scientists?

In the past the effects of
prenatal video imprinting were
somewhat random, since every-
body by necessity watched a
variety of TV shows. Now,
however, a VCR and a decent tape
library create the exciting pos-
sibility of actually molding the
personality of your child in a

predictable way by a regimen of constant, selective viewing through pregnancy and even into the delivery room (if your hospital is sufficiently enlightened).

Want your child to be a doctor? View hour after hour of *General Hospital, Marcus Welby, Ben Casey, Dr. Kildare* and *Trapper John, M.D.* Want a world-class athlete? Hope you can stand megahours of Howard Cosell. An intellectual? Stay tuned to PBS. A musician? Subscribe to MTV and watch tapes of Lawrence Welk, the Monkees, the Archies and the ends of those *Ozzie and Harriet* episodes when Ricky sings. The President of the United States? View a steady diet of westerns and other B-movies.

Just one warning. Be very careful to determine exactly what you want your child to become and view only those shows—or parts of shows—that will encourage that development. One hapless woman decided she wanted a wacky, redheaded baby girl so she watched hour after hour of *I Love Lucy.* She was surprised to give birth to a dark-haired baby boy whose first word was "Bobalu!"

Infant Viewing: Nourished by the Glass Teat

That infants are attracted to movement and sound is attested to by the hundreds of mobiles designed to mount on their cribs. But how many thousands of times can an infant watch little pieces of plastic spinning in slow circles to the tune of Brahm's "Lullaby" or "Teddy Bear's Picnic" before it drives the baby buggy?

Television has also earned the sobriquet "Boob Tube" because of its nurturing influence on all ages—especially the young.

No, better to mount a small Watchman-style Television above the crib. With constantly changing visual images and extra hours of exposure to spoken language, your child will have a perceptual head start on his or her peers, especially if you keep the set tuned to a variety of programming. Don't make the mistake of tuning in *Sesame Street* and other so-called educational programs. While these might be good for teaching specific skills (e.g. saying the alphabet or consuming large quantities of cookies), at this stage you want to expose your child to a general overview of the diversity of the world, from the gunplay of *Remington Steele* to the foreplay of *Dynasty.*

Mounted correctly, the same TV can easily be moved to baby's carseat, high chair, playpen and stroller for continuous Television stimulation. This toy is cheap at any price: the benefits to your child will never be outgrown.

You can improvise a lot of child care video paraphernalia simply from household wire and a Sony Watchman.

The Electronic Hearth

"The family that views together, renews together."

—Dr. Davenport Spudd

Cherish those hours of family viewing time . . .

Polls show that, aside from eating, watching TV together is the most popular family activity. Emotions glow warmer than an old picture tube when the whole family sits in front of the TV with gallons of Kool-Ade, tubs of Orville Redenbacher's finest smothered in Squeeze Parkay and a gross of generic chocolate chip cookies. Who can forget the family discussions during commercials and station breaks? Who can forget the screams, the taunts, the good-natured melees about what to watch?

Smart families keep extra TV sets around the house for those times when they cannot agree. However, they make sure that the extra TVs are not as good as the number one screen. Second-hand black-and-white sets with 9-inch screens and coat-hanger antennae that require an occasional bang on the side are perfect. This arrangement grudgingly accommodates individual viewing needs while encouraging family members back toward the Electronic Hearth in the living room.

. . . Television can create the strongest of family ties.

TV Family Therapy

Beaver: Boy, when I get to be a father, I'm not gonna yell at my kids.
Wally: Sure you will. The only fathers that don't yell at their kids are on Television.

It is an unfortunate fact that few of us are lucky enough to have families as wonderful as those portrayed on Television. Many of us, young and old alike, feel cheated by what nature has given us in the way of families. But now we can stop sniveling about the shortcomings of our parents, children and spouses, according to Dr. Davenport Spudd, Couch Potato adviser, and choose new ones from the rich variety of characters on TV.

"Who hasn't wished for a mother like June Cleaver, a spouse like Kate Jackson or Thomas Magnum and kids like Gary Coleman or Pebbles Flintstone?" asks the good doctor. "Most people spend more time interacting with their favorite characters on TV than with the members of their family anyway, so it's just a matter of adopting the right ones."

In choosing your TV family you should do more than just find characters who fill the deficiencies in your real family, Dr. Spudd points out. "It doesn't do any good to find the ideal TV father if he's on a series that gets cancelled mid-season. In fact, it could cause serious psychological problems." He suggests choosing characters that look like they'll be around for episode after episode and using a video recorder to make sure you have access to your new family members at all hours and for years to come.

He has found children especially responsive to TV parents. "Sometimes a single mother will find her task easier if she has a cache of tapes handy of her favorite surrogate husband. One of my clients has tapes of Ward Cleaver cataloged so if one of her kids skips school, for example, she can put on the appropriate cassette and Ward can cuss out her kid along with the Beaver."

Dr. Spudd recommends the following TV characters as especially appropriate surrogate parents:

Ages 1-3. Fathers: Fred Flintstone, Ben Cartwright, Alfred Hitchcock, Howard Cosell. Mothers: Jayne Kennedy, Samantha Stevens, Jane Jetson, Ethel Mertz.

Ages 3-7. Fathers: Ward Cleaver, Sgt. Bilko, Ed Norton, Dan Rather. Mothers: Edith Bunker, Diana Prince, Miss Jane Pittman, Lucy Ricardo.

Ages 7-12. Fathers: Uncle Fester, Jack LaLanne, Mean Joe Greene, Groucho Marx. Mothers: Ann Romero, Mary Hartman, Agent 99, Madge the Manicurist.

Ages 12-20. Fathers: Foster Brooks, J. R. Ewing, Perry Mason, Napoleon Solo. Mothers: Julia Child, Joan Rivers, Mrs. Olson, My Mother the Car.

Ages 20+. Fathers: Captain Kangaroo, Mr. T, Jimmy Swaggert, Barney Fife. Mothers: Barbara Woodhouse, Hazel, Miss Brooks, Louise Jefferson.

Membership Poll:
The Perfect Substitute TV Family

In response to an invitation to "stop sniveling about the less-than-perfect family you were given and choose the family you would have liked to have," several hundred subscribers of *The Tuber's Voice*, the Couch Potato newsletter, chose the following:

Father

The number one choice for the most appropriate dad was **Ozzie Nelson**. Reasons ranged from "He never got excited" to "I want to do the same job he never did."

Ward Cleaver came in as a very close second—"He always knows what to say" and "So I could inherit his shirts."

- **Walter Cronkite**—"He knows what's going on."
- **James Beresford Tipton** (*The Millionaire*)—"The money, only the money."
- **Capt. Video**—"So we could go for spaceship rides."
- **Number Six** (*The Prisoner*)—"Superior genetic material."
- **Jack LaLanne**—"So strong."
- **Percy Dovetonsils**—"Good looks, charm, charisma."
- **Bentley Gregg** (*Bachelor Father*)—"He had a good job and Peter the houseboy."
- **Joe E. Ross as Gronk** (*It's About Time*)—"Great to have a dad that stupid."
- **John Steed** (*The Avengers*)—"Nothing bothers him and he could pass on survival skills necessary for any life I chose."
- **Maynard G. Krebs**—"I wouldn't have to work."

Mother

Gracie Allen was mentioned most often as the most desirable TV mother figure. Some of the reasons: "She'd give me a unique outlook," "Life would be fun" and "She'd never know how fucked-up I was getting."

- **June Cleaver**—"Most sympathetic" "Submissive."
- **June Lockhart** (*Lassie, Lost in Space*)—"She had lots of experience as a TV mom."
- **Mrs. Olsen** (Folger's coffee ads)—"Generous to a fault."
- **Annette Funicello**—"Peanut butter and a purple Thunderbird ...Oh Mama!"
- **Ethel Mertz**—"Ready for anything" "Nonjudgmental."
- **Ginger Grant** (*Gilligan's Island*)—"Great wardrobe."

Siblings

- **Wally Cleaver**—"A self-effacing-type dude."
- **Kathy "Kitten" Anderson**—"I wouldn't have to feel guilty about hating my sister."
- **Bobbie Jo, Billie Jo and Betty Jo** (*Petticoat Junction*)—"I like the middle name Jo."
- **Beaver Cleaver**—"To have a brother dumber than me."
- Mr. Peabody's boy, **Sherman**—"Great straight man."
- **Eddie Haskell** and **Rollo Larson** (*Sanford and Son*)—"They could get me a good price on a color TV."

Wife

- **Ellie Mae Clampett**—"Rich, gorgeous, dumb."

- **Jeannie** (Barbara Eden)—"She lived to please her master."
- **June Cleaver**—"I want pearls dragged through my oatmeal."
- **Emma Peel**—"Great looks and brains."
- **Charo**—"I understand she's quite 'talented.' "

Husband

- **John Beresford Tipton**—"He's rich and you never see him."
- **Gomez Addams**—"I love arm kissing."
- **Tristan Rogers**—"Probably a good lay."
- **Mick Belker** (*Hill St. Blues*)—"I like being bitten."

Grandfather

- **Amos McCoy**—"Who would question Walter Brennan?" "He wouldn't be able to read the police report."
- **Mr. Wizard**—"So I could have fun in his laboratory."
- **Floyd the Barber**—"Free haircuts, wit and wisdom."
- **Little Ricky**—"It would mean I was very young."
- **Grandpa Munster**—"For arcane occult knowledge and powers, also for vaudeville routines."

Grandmother

Granny Clampett from *The Beverly Hillbillies* got the most votes for grandmother. Here are some of the reasons: "Spring Tonic," "Dinner on the pool table," "She didn't take shit from anyone, including the U.S. government." Other favorites:

- **Aunt Bea**—"Her homemade pies and advice."
- **Jane Pauley**—"I want a grandmother who keeps up with current events."
- **Mrs. Davis** (*Our Miss Brooks*)—"Not too much advice."
- **Julia Child**—"When I visited her, she'd feed me" "Sunday dinner."
- **Loni Anderson**—"People would stare."

Uncle

- **Uncle Fester**—"Human light bulb."
- **Rod Serling**—"Intellectual stimulation."
- **Frank Nitti** (*Untouchables*)—"Source of explosives and arms."

Aunt

- **Aunt Bea**—"Good cookin' if not good lookin'."
- **Betty White**—"She would keep family events, especially funerals, in the right perspective."

Children

- All of the **Cartwright Boys**—"Handy in a fight."
- **Gary Coleman**—"Large income" "Wouldn't have to buy him clothes too often since he doesn't grow much."
- **Ellie Mae Clampett**—"Bad girl, bringing all those animals in here...I'll have to spank you."
- **Johnny Carson**—"To support me."
- **Bam-Bam Rubble, Rusty Hamer, Cindy Brady** and **Larry Mondello**—"I'd demand that they entertain the hell out of me."

Neighbors

- The Coneheads
- Thorny Thorndike
- The Addams Family

Pets

- **Tennessee Tuxedo**—"What could be better than a talking penguin?"
- **Spot** (*The Munsters*)—"He'd keep undesirables out of the neighborhood."
- **Baretta's Cockatoo** and **Morris the Cat**—"They're neat-o."
- **Cleo** the Basset Hound (*People's Choice*)—"Pithy wit and great hiccup."
- **Jethro Bodine**—"To crush people on command."
- **Arnold** (the pig) **Ziffel**

The VHF Years: 2 to 13

The VHF years—so named because they correspond with the numbers on the VHF knob and because kids often view with a Very High Frequency — are developmentally important for the growing Tuber because 75 percent of everything you'll ever learn you learned before the age of seven. Since nothing compacts information and life experience as densely as Television, it's reassuring that the average 5-year-old has already invested more time in front of the Tube than a college student will spend in four years of classes, that an average child will manage to get in 17,040 hours of TV before graduation despite 11,000 hours wasted in the classroom.

Some children may be tempted by an unhealthy attraction to outdoor activities.

While this 17,040 hours comes out to 710 full days, over 10 percent of their lives, children are sometimes deprived of the carefree, guiltless viewing that is every person's birthright. School, restrictive parents, outdated religious prohibitions, an unhealthy attraction to outdoor activities and inadequate video equipment all limit a child's viewing potential.

Not to mention the alarmists. There are many groups concerned about kids' watching TV violence, TV sex, TV commercials—even *Sesame Street* and Disney! The anti-TV fanatics had an orgy of doomsaying a few years ago when a pollster asked kindergarteners, "Which do you like better, TV or Daddy?" and 54 percent said, "TV!"

(This follows their alarm a few years before when a different poll showed that owing to Television's influence, more children recognized Ronald McDonald than the President, Santa Claus, or any other entity, real or mythical.)

As Couch Potatoes we think the only real surprise is that Daddy did as well as he did. After all, what can a father do? Maybe a few card tricks and a bad Cagney imitation, at best. How can this compare with the wonders of TV: Bugs Bunny! *I Love Lucy* reruns! The A-Team! Smurfs! Big Bird! And much, much more!

TV and Violence

Does TV viewing cause violence in children? This serious charge gives pause even to parents who should know better.

And the debate's having a terrible effect on children's programming. Programmers, timid in the face of organized big-money pressure mobs and skittish advertisers, now decline to broadcast anything that isn't socially positive, constructive and conducive to peaceful co-operation with the established order. In other words, most of the great kid-vid shows from the past like *Howdy Doody, Zorro* and *Soupy Sales* would never pass muster. Even the classic Warner Brothers cartoons— Tweety, Sylvester, Road-runner, Bugs Bunny, Daffy Duck and the rest—are being mangled by the censor to excise "objectionable" material.

This is inexcusable. Even the so-called experts, traditionally hostile to TV, have been unable to come up with unambiguous evidence of harm to children from watching violent programming.

In fact, the most damning of the studies, if interpreted correctly, proves that TV actually *prevents* violence among children.

The researchers watched a group of children at play. They wheeled in a TV and let the children watch. After a while they made the kids stop watching and return to their play. The researchers counted the number of aggressive acts during each period. The graph shows the results.

Since aggressive acts increased slightly after the kids watched TV, the researchers concluded that TV causes violence. But does it? Any rational person looking at this graph would conclude the opposite. If TV viewing causes violence, why was there virtually none while the kids were viewing? This study obviously proves that TV viewing *prevents* violence.

And clearly there were more aggressive acts after viewing than before because the kids were forced to *stop* watching TV. That would make *anybody* mad.

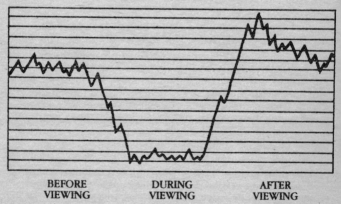

NUMBER OF AGGRESSIVE ACTS

| BEFORE VIEWING | DURING VIEWING | AFTER VIEWING |

The Tater Tots*

Couch Potato parents cannot always be there to make sure their kids are viewing properly every day. One solution is to find an unemployed neighbor who will, for an appropriate amount of beer, view with your child.

Even better is to sign your kid up with the Tater Tots, the Couch Potato junior auxiliary, which acts as advocate for the viewing tastes of children and teaches them crucial viewing skills they'll need later in life.

Couch Potato lodges often adopt dens of Tater Tots in a special program we call Big Brother Is Watching With You. Older Tubers take time to help their "small fries" earn merit badges in viewing skills from the esoteric to the practical, from how to see the future in your TV

*Not to be confused with the potato products of the same name manufactured by Ore-Ida Foods and cherished by Couch Potatoes everywhere for their tastiness and ease of preparation.

screen to how to make the perfect Coffee Crystal Sandwich. In return the Tots adjust the sets and fetch food and drink for their elders, serving an important need long neglected since the day Couch Tomatoes discovered Women's Lib.

Late at night, the lights and audio go down and the kids toast a few hundred marshmallows and s'mores in the toaster oven while the older viewers recap scary episodes from *The Outer Limits* and *The Twilight Zone*.

As the TVs flicker in the darkness, young Tater Tots sometimes raise their voices in song. Since they see many more than the 20,000 yearly commercials average for their age, the Tots memorize new jingles by the hundreds and love to sing them. Some nights their Big Brothers teach classic commercial jingles from the past, which is why, in schoolyards around the country, you occasionally hear strains of "Every Parliament gives you/Extra margin..." and "Call Roto-Rooter/ That's the name..." instead of traditional playsongs and jumprope ditties, as kids use these tunes—America's only truly original musical form —to soothe the schoolday anguish of being separated from Television.

A viewer from the early days passes on a legacy.

Children's Viewing Rights

1. Children have the inalienable right to life, Mr. T and the pursuit of Television.

2. If children can con-
vince their parents
that they are too sick
to go to school, they
have earned the right
to watch
TV all day
without
fear of
make-up schoolwork.

3. While children should be free to view without exploita-
tion or unreasonable interruption, asking them to earn
their keep by changing the channel, fetching you a beer
or running out for pizza makes them feel like trusted and
responsible human beings and should be done often.

*Asking children to help with the chores makes them
feel like trusted, responsible human beings.*

4. Depriving a child of Television is a form of child abuse. It can lead to Telecastration Anxiety and Zenith Envy, both serious psychosexual problems. Children of parents who prevent viewing should be encouraged to run away from home and become NBC pages.

Telecastration Anxiety begins at home.

5. May this be the generation that never has to hear these crippling parental injunctions and put-downs:

    "You're wasting your life in front of that damned Boob Tube!"

    "It's a beautiful day. Turn off that TV and get some sunshine."

    "How can you watch this stuff?"

    "Why don't you read a book?"

    "You'll go blind!"

    "No TV tonight unless . . ."

Advice to Couch Potato Teens:
Straight Answers to the Earnest Questions of TV-viewing Youth

By Dr. Davenport H. Spudd, PBS

Note: Dr. Spudd, Couch Potato advice expert and world-renowned authority on TV psychotherapy, is the originator of Gilligan Therapy and other innovative viewing techniques. He has graciously consented to discuss some common teen concerns.

Dear Teenagers:

You're at an awkward age, making the difficult transition from the childhood tastes of Saturday morning cartoons to sophisticated adult fare like *Gilligan's Island, Laverne and Shirley, The A-Team* and *The Dukes of Hazzard.* During this awkward time you are susceptible to unhealthy alternatives to wholesome TV viewing: drugs, religious cults, homework, promiscuous sex, sports, video games and extracurricular clubs.

I hear you crying out for sanity in a world gone mad. I see you searching for someone wise to guide you. Someone like me, Dr. Davenport Spudd.

Family Problems

Dear Dr. Spudd:
What's wrong with parents nowadays, anyway?

Parents who ignore TV's role models may find themselves hopelessly out of touch.

Plenty. Most never grew up. I blame that in part on today's TV programming. Where are the wise, all-knowing parental role models of yesteryear like Ward and June Cleaver, Ozzie and Harriet Nelson, Jim and Margaret Anderson, and Sheriff Andy Taylor? Parents today, on TV and off, are usually naive imbeciles who know less than their kids. I suggest a law that requires all prospective parents to watch hundreds of hours of the great TV moms and dads before being allowed to bring children into the world.

Dear Dr. Spudd:

My parents watch TV constantly. We live in a small house and they play it so loud I can't get away from it. What should I do?

I realize you're at an age where rebellion against your parents is natural. Still, this is one area where Father and Mother know best. They know that nothing beats TV for compressing life experiences. More happens in every half hour of TV programming than in weeks or months of normal living. Your parents, as a result, have vicariously absorbed the experience of a thousand lifetimes. Don't throw away all that accumulated wisdom.

TV Dating

Dear Dr. Spudd:

I want to invite my girlfriend over to watch TV with my family, but my parents won't let me. Does this seem fair to you?

No, but look at it from their point of view. Some parents consider TV viewing

to be a very private pleasure to be shared only with immediate family.

Other parents find it awkward to view with dating teens because fidgeting, whispering and giggling can be distracting to serious viewers. Perhaps you can assure your parents that, should you and your date feel compelled toward any distracting activities, you will take it upon yourselves to move quietly into a more secluded area of the house, like your bedroom.

Dear Dr. Spudd:
Watching TV all the time is fun, but on a date I don't just want to hang around the house with my parents and brothers and sisters.

That's understandable. And, thanks to the new little portable sets, you and your date can go to the beach, the malt shop or the high

school hop with the confidence that you won't miss a minute of *Dallas*.

Or why not take your date to your local Sears for the evening? You'll find dozens of sets to simulview to your hearts' content. And most Sears stores place the refreshment stand conveniently near the TV department.

TV and Sex

Dear Dr. Spudd:
I'm a 16-year-old girl. I know you don't approve of teen drug use, but how about teen sex?

No, thanks, not today. I have a

headache. Try Chef Aldo.

Dear Dr. Spudd:
My girlfriend wears designer everything. Even underclothes. Even though I'm a Couch Potato, and not naive, I never knew of such things before. What do you think?

I'm surprised that you think there's anything strange about that. As a TV viewer you surely must be accustomed to commercial interruptions during the best parts of the action.

Dear Dr. Spudd:
Can you get pregnant from watching Love Boat?

I think it's criminal that in this latter part of the twentieth century there are still teens growing up without adequate sex education. Can you imagine in this day and age a girl growing up afraid she might get pregnant from watching *Love Boat?* Shocking!

Now, to answer your question: no, you cannot get pregnant from simply watching *Love Boat.* It's physiologically impossible.

You can, however, get pregnant from watching *Magnum P.I.*

Music Video

Dear Dr. Spudd:
   Is MTV financed by a secret cabal of Presbyterians? Can rock video cause brain damage? Can it make you want to put your pet poodle in the microwave?

No, to all your questions. Those are just rumors. I suspect they are being spread by parents to scare kids away from the Tube so they themselves can watch *Hill Street Blues* and *Dallas.*

Equipment Fears

Dear Dr. Spudd:
   I'm a guy 13 years old. Sometimes I think my equipment is smaller than normal. I'm embarrassed by how small it is.

You needn't be. Although you're at an age when making comparisons with your friends is not uncommon, remember that the size of your TV screen has nothing to do with its ability to give pleasure. As we used to say when I was young: "Anything more than an eyeful is wasted."

Dear Dr. Spudd:
   I have a bad case of acne. What can I do?

Watch more TV. For your acne, sit close to a color set at least twelve hours a day with the red and blue tints turned extra high. The rays from a color TV can also be used to regulate menstrual cycles, cure hyperactivity, increase hormonal production, prevent tooth decay and sharpen razor blades.

Dear Dr. Spudd:
   I'd like to watch more TV, but I'm very weight-conscious. I'm afraid the inactivity and Couch Potato diet would make me fat. Isn't that right?

No. Most Couch Potatoes aren't fat; instead they have a robust, healthy bottom-heavy weight distribution which is perfect for Prolonged Viewing since it serves the function of both padding and ballast.

Dear Dr. Spudd:
   Sometimes I feel anxious and depressed for no reason. Can Prolonged TV Viewing make me a happier person?

Yes, of course. TV viewing relaxes you. If you watch enough you'll be happier, more at ease and more confident in yourself. The effects are so striking that many people call prolonged viewing "Transcendental Vegetation."

Twelve Things Dr. Spudd Wishes He Had Known When He Was a Teenager

1. Friends may come, friends may go, but your TV will never desert you.

2. It's not *what* you watch that's important, it's *how* and *how much* you watch.

3. You'll have reached maturity when you again start liking the TV programs you scorned as a teen for being "too childish."

4. Do not befoul your own viewing space.

5. The undying love and respect of younger siblings is yours if you take the time to view with them.

6. Changing the channel will not solve the problem if the problem is within you.

7. I cried because I had no VCR until I met a man who had no TV at all.

8. Judge not another human until you have reclined for a day in his viewing chair.

9. The screen is always darkest before the next program begins.

10. Art imitates life, but life imitates TV.

11. Go your own path: the laugh track does not always know what's funniest.

12. If you're not willing to watch an occasional soap opera or football game, you're not ready for a serious relationship.

TV Party Games for Teens

■ *Space Invaders:* When the commercial begins everyone on the couch tries to "invade each others' space." Object: to be the last person remaining on the couch.

■ *Soundtrack:* Turn down the sound and provide your own dialogue and sound effects.

■ *"Winkie Dink" Art:* Provide water-soluable paints and crayons and allow your friends to draw on the TV screen.

■ *Target Shoot:* Invest in dart guns and shoot at your least favorite TV characters. Or wet some tissue paper and throw the glops at the screen. Give points for direct hits on agreed-upon targets.

Potato Pets

Pets are man's second-best friends; maybe that's why they seem strangely indifferent to friend number one—Television. But there's no reason why they can't be taught an appreciation of TV programming.

Cats, for instance, are very visually oriented, so they'll often watch anything with a lot of movement. They especially enjoy shows with rodents, birds, fish and other felines, but stay clear of certain cartoons like *Mighty Mouse* or *Tom & Jerry* which portray cats in a negative stereotype.

Dogs rely more heavily on their sensitive ears and noses. Still, your dog will share the joy of viewing with you if you watch shows with animal sound effects like *Grizzley Adams* or *Tarzan*. Many enjoy seeing their peers in action on *Lassie* and *Huckleberry Hound*. Car-chasers seem to like *The Dukes of Hazzard* and *Knight Rider*. If none of these appeal to your canine, try rubbing your TV set with raw hamburger.

Other animals like birds and fish find it a treat to see shows that remind them of their natural environs. For fish, put the TV next to the bowl whenever *Jacques Cousteau* or *Seahunt* get rerun; for birds, try *Sky King* and *Superman*.

Late Show:
The Post-Prime Time Years (65+)

Couch Potatoes have great respect for the true elders of the viewing world. Older viewers (sometimes called Rockin' Chair

Couch Tomato Lodge #342: The Cable Grams,
Springhill Nursing Home, Springhill, Ohio

The venerable Rockin' Chair Potatoes can teach us much about the beauties of the sedentary existence.

Potatoes or Senior Sitter-zens) are venerated for their ability to sit almost motionless for lengthy periods of time and watch practically anything that's on the set. Having absorbed decades of Television programming, many have achieved a quiet oneness with their electronic companions.

Old enough to remember the years before Philo T. Farnsworth invented Television as we know it, back when TV was just a wistful dream of science-fiction writers, senior viewers have been permanently affected by their deprivation. Growing up without Television created a "video deficiency" that older viewers are still trying to overcome.

Older women are especially dedicated. As a group they watch the most TV—an average of 41 hours and 13 minutes per week, 10½ hours more than is typical. When asked in a survey how they would most like to spend two hours alone with their husbands, older women most commonly answered watching TV ("making love" was a distant second).

This kind of commitment puts many younger viewers to shame. Yet older Americans are not always well served by Television programmers. Where are the great TV role models of the past like Granny of the *Beverly Hillbillies,* Amos McCoy and Fred Sanford? Why aren't more stations rerunning Lawrence Welk? It seems we owe better to our older viewers.

The Ravages of Aging

Despite the benefits of aging to Tubers—older people need less sleep, for instance, leaving that much more viewing time—it has its difficulties, too.

■ *Forgetfulness:* Short-term memory is more degraded by age than long-term memory, which explains why you can remember all four networks' Thursday night lineup for the 1951-52 season, yet have difficulty remembering what you saw last night, or even where you left the remote control.

■ *Fading eyesight:* Colors and clarity sometimes fade in later years. While buying a bigger screen and turning the brightness control higher help, some older viewers invest in picture tubes specially ground to their glasses prescriptions.

■ *Hearing problems:* Hearing aids only partially solve hearing difficulties since they amplify more than just the TV soundtrack, including humming appliances, roaring traffic and annoying conversations. Better to turn your TV's volume way up to drown out these annoying noises (as well as the sound of your neighbors yelling and pounding on your walls in the middle of the night).

■ *Poor circulation:* Cold hands and feet can be helped by watching exercise programs—especially those featuring attractive bodies in skimpy clothing.

■ *Arthuritis:* This is more a mental difficulty than a physical one, characterized by a profoundly debilitating nostalgia for times past when the airwaves were populated by people named Arthur—Godfrey, Murray, Linkletter, Carney and the rest. There is no known cure.

Sign Off

Couch Potato Death Benefits

The Planted Potato Option:

Who says you can't take it with you? The cold, cold ground doesn't seem nearly as chilling when you know you'll be buried with your own Television set, featuring an Eternal Picture Tube that will stay lit forever. Have it set to the channel of your choice, or better yet, have it equipped with a remote control so your loved ones can change the channel for you when they come to visit. Satellite dish, VCR or cable hookup available at additional cost.

The Baked Potato Option:

Your remains will be cremated in Julia Child's oven and your ashes will be scattered over your choice of Fantasy Island, Gilligan's Island, either of the Beaver's houses, the Ewings' Estate, Falcon Crest Winery, Gotham City, Fernwood, Peyton Place, Route 66, 77 Sunset Strip, Fawlty Towers, the Ponderosa, Kate and Luke McCoy's ranch, Green Acres, Hooterville, Mayberry or over 200 other locations.

Some have chosen to be immortalized with video tapes of themselves played at their resting place.

The Stuffed Potato Option:

Spend eternity the way you spent your life: lounging among your Couchmates in your local Couch Potato lodge, watching TV. Thanks to new advances in taxidermy, your body can be comfortably positioned in your favorite easy chair long after your spirit has hopped the soul train.

The Planted Potato Option.

Biography of an Avid Viewer

Virgil was deprived of Television in his early years. His parents were bibliophiles and wouldn't allow a TV in their home.

IT'S CALLED AN IDIOT BOX, SON.

HEY, DAD!! LOOK AT THIS THING CAN WE GET ONE?

COME ALONG WE'RE LATE FOR THE LIBRARY MEETING

Lou's TV and APPLIANCE

Things began to change when the neighbors got a set.

THERE ARE PEOPLE SQUIRTING EACH OTHER WITH SELTZER BOTTLES NEXT DOOR.

SHH... PLEASE BE QUIET, SON.

OH, THAT'S NICE, DEAR

He spent an increasing amount of time at the homes of friends who had TVs, catching up on all of the great shows he'd been missing.

SORRY, VIRGIL, BUT JIMMY IS STAYING AT HIS UNCLE'S FOR THE WEEKEND.

UH, NO PROBLEM, BECAUSE I DECIDED TO STAY HERE FOR THE NEXT MONTH OR SO.

Soon TV entities, such as Froggy the Gremlin and Cecil the Seasick Sea Serpent, began to dominate his consciousness.

He didn't waste any time obtaining his own personal TV set.

TV programming provided Virgil with a rich source of information, often helping him with his studies.

Naturally, he had to make a few social sacrifices as watching TV became his all-consuming pastime.

Unfortunately, Virgil's folks didn't approve of his growing love of TV, and sent him to a special summer camp for sedentary youth.

The camp's TV deprogramming methods had little effect on him.

Virgil's parents eventually accepted his love of TV.

Years later he was on his own in a modest apartment, living a spartan, yet satisfying life of advanced Couch Potatoism.

His girlfriend, Dotty, shared his enthusiasm for Tubing. Together they soaked up an enormous amount of blue light.

He took her advice and got on the show. Soon he was doing great.

He had no problem coming up with the winning answers.

Virgil and Dotty married and spent his fortune on the most sophisticated video equipment available, including a custom-built simulviewing center.

After a few years of marital and video bliss, a couple of Tater Tots appeared on the scene. A happy ending seemed inevitable. Well, almost...

TV FACTS

☐ Mr. Potatohead was the first toy advertised on TV.

☐ Another reason to let your kids watch "adult" programming: there's six time less violence than on Saturday morning cartoons.

☐ U.S. households with personal computers watch 40% less TV.

☐ When in 1977 the *Detroit Free Press* sadistically attempted to bribe families to give up TV for a month for $500, they had to approach 120 families to find five who would accept the challenge.

☐ You burn 1½ calories per minute while watching TV—50% more than while sleeping.

☐ If you could wrestle them away from their owners, you could make a line from San Francisco to New York with all the VCRs now in American homes.

☐ Television avoiders and phobics make up 5-6% of the U.S. population.

☐ Prime time TV characters are over 50 times more likely to be involved in a violent confrontation than people who reside on this side of the screen.

☐ Couch Potatoes in space! NASA's Ames Research Center in Mountain View, California, issued a report in 1983 questioning the suitability of the young and athletic for space travel because of the complications tight muscles and flexible arteries present in gravity-free flight. Better, said one researcher, would be "a typical sedentary, middle-aged slob" with a touch of arteriosclerosis and high blood pressure.

TV and Food:
Couchside Cuisine from Chef Aldo, the Station Break Gourmet

Chef Aldo, Couch Potato Snackmaster, was one of the first to realize the importance of continuous nutrition while viewing. His concept of "Nouvelle Set-Side Sustenance" has been grudgingly recognized by food experts everywhere as being in a class by itself. Aldo's godfather—strange but true, we swear on a stack of TV Guides—was the husband of the late health food writer Adelle Davis.

Despite this era of fad diets and obsessive dietary concerns, Tubers are returning to the high-fat, low-fiber diet so conducive to good viewing. it's been said that an army travels on its stomach, and so do the great legions of Couch Potatoes on the front lines of the video revolution. Without leaving our comfy chairs, without investing in kitchen tools any more expensive than a secondhand set-side toaster oven, we can make tantalizing "viewing fuel" in the time of a single commercial cluster. But before we sink our teeth into some recipes, let's review two important concepts:

■ *Squeezine:* The use of squeeze, spray and aerosol containers for quick tube-side dining without (much) mess or the need to take your eyes off the screen.

■ *Nutritional Assemblage:* Like a well-built viewing room, the Couch Potato fare is constructed by assembling basic components:

1. *The Foundation* supports the other ingredients. Good ones include white bread, taco shells, pizza crust, pita bread and ice cream cones. Because it is edible, the foundation obviates the need for plates and flatware.

2. *The Body* usually consists of meat products and by-products; it's comparable to the bricks of a building in importance.

3. *The Binder* acts like mortar sticking together chunks that might otherwise end up in your lap. The category includes Hershey's chocolate sauce, relishes, condiments, aerosol Cheez-Whiz or the old standby, Squeeze Parkay.

4. *The Topping* is usually a nondairy product from a tub or aerosol can, but may include anything that gives a decorative, nutritional edge to the food you've prepared. Especially useful when you need to cover something up that didn't quite come out the way it was supposed to.

You'll see how these principles apply in the recipes that follow. Once you get the basic idea, you will develop the confidence to concoct your own specialties.

Celebrated food guru Chef Aldo proposes a toast for proper set-side snacking.

Toast

The classic foundation for any set-side meal is white bread toast. Couch Potatoes regard it as one of the major food groups, along with salt, grease, sugar, alcohol and caffeine. We feel a kinship with bleached flour, since it matches the Prolonged Viewing life-style perfectly: both are highly refined by the best of modern technology.

The classic binder for toast recipes has long been Squeeze Parkay margarine. With a conventional toaster oven, you can lube your slices before, after or even during toasting, depending on whether you want that health-giving grease *in* or *on top of* the bread.

Once you've piled enough stuff on top of your white bread, you have appetizer, main course and dessert all rolled into one! For example:

Breaktoast

White bread
Powdered eggs
Tang instant breakfast drink
Bac-Os imitation bacon bits
Instant mashed potatoes
salt, pepper, ketchup
Squeeze Parkay

Toast bread, apply Parkay liberally. To lower left corner of toast sprinkle Bac-Os; to lower right corner pour a heaping tablespoon of Tang powder. Cover remainder of toast surface with instant mashed potato flakes and powdered eggs. Season to taste.

All that's missing is that morning coffee—this can be remedied with a Coffee Crystal Sandwich (to toast add Parkay, Folger's instant coffee crystals, artificial creamer and sugar or NutraSweet to taste).

Turkey Toast Tubs

White bread
Ketchup, mustard with
**   horseradish, salt, pepper**
Turkey meat hot dog
Squeeze Parkay

Stack three slices of bread and mold them with moderate hand pressure into the shape of a satellite dish. Shred turkey frank with scissors and fill the dish. Garnish heavily with ketchup and mustard and pinch bread into pouch around it. Glaze with Squeeze Parkay and pop into oven until golden brown. Serve hot.

Another demonstration of the versatility of the toast motif is this all-purpose food and medicinal drug product—an elixir for much that ails the hard-viewing, hard-living Couch Potato.

Head Toast (Popularly Known as The Toast of the Town)

White bread
Squeeze Parkay
Powdered Alka-Seltzer
Powered Kool-Ade (any flavor)

Toast bread, splatter with Parkay. Sprinkle package of Alka-Seltzer on top and flavor with Kool-Ade crystals. Perfect in the late evening to round out a day of Toasting.

Pizza: Ethnic Toast?

When you get right down to it, what is pizza dough if not raw toast? That's why so many toast recipes can, with a little tomato sauce, aerosol cheese analog and assorted spices, be adapted to pizza. But the following recipe only works with pizza dough. It is unique in that it is not just a food, but a bib and placemat as well.

Sloppy Seconds Pizza

Frozen pizza crust
Snackmate or Cheez-Whiz aerosol
    cheese food
Deplorable eating habits

Make a thick ring of cheese food around the edge of the pizza crust. Lay the crust on your lap while you view and snack. After several hours the crust will be covered with a thick layer of food residue from your snack spillage. Bake in toaster oven until crust is browned.

Built-in Sauce Pouch Treats

Sometimes you can find ready-made pouches with sauces already included. This first assemblage is based on that most pleasing conveyance of vital nutrients, the jelly doughnut.

Tunuts

Can of tuna in oil
Large jelly doughnut (strawberry,
**   raspberry or lemon)**
Cola
Topping of choice

Holding doughnut with injection hole up, snip off top 1/3 with clean scissors, discard into mouth of self or couch companion. Scoop out half of the jelly with finger, then pack cavity to capacity with tuna. Sprinkle with your favorite cola and add the topping of your choice (recommended: marshmallow creme or butterscotch syrup).

Here is an elegant continental fish specialty, based on the ever-popular Hostess Fruit Pie, with a variation for those who are more ambitious and demanding in their food-prep standards.

Hostess Fish Citron

Frozen fish sticks
Hostess individual lemon pie
Best Foods or Hellman's Tartar Sauce
Package of Beer Nuts

Heat a fish stick to slightly below room temperature, but do not allow to become too soft or crumbly. Break hole in one end of pie's crust, just large enough to insert fish stick. Insert fish stick carefully.

Bake the pie in your toaster oven at medium temperature until glaze begins to liquefy. Sliver a dozen beer nuts with clean scissors and sprinkle on pie crust. Return to oven until beer nuts toast slightly. Add tartar sauce and serve.

Serving variation: To Anglicize this dish, substitute a butterscotch pie for the lemon pie.

Eager-eating Couch Potatoes always perk up when they hear the announcement that the snack is being prepared from scratch. That extra effort and dedication means a lot, and it really doesn't take much time. Here's a truly homemade version of the Hostess Fish Citron.

Fish Citron *(from scratch)*

Fish sticks
Arabian pita (pocket) bread
Lemon-flavored Jell-O
Tartar sauce
Beer Nuts

Snip off 1/4 of the pita bread and discard. Open the bread by blowing into it. Mix lemon Jell-O according to package instructions and fill pita pouch 2/3 full. Allow to congeal in refrigerator several hours.

Cook fish sticks in toaster over and force into Jell-O. Smother in tartar sauce and garnish with slivered Beer Nuts. Voilà! A made-from-scratch delicacy *a la Français* that will insure your legendary status as Snackmaster in your lodge.

Handy tip: If you make your citrons large it helps to double shell (putting one pita bread inside another like double-bagging groceries).

Here's a basic sauce that will stick to the ribs, or to anything else. It's a favorite on my TV tray because it is so versatile.

Soda Roux

Can of favorite soft drink
Nondairy creamer

Empty soda can into nonstick saucepan and bring to a boil over stove or Sterno can. Lower heat and simmer until much of the liquid has boiled away and soda residue is about the consistency of Mrs. Butterworth's Syrup. Thicken with nondairy creamer to desired consistency, anywhere from that of a multigrade motor oil to Pla-Doh, depending on your purposes. Its flexibility makes this sauce perfect for any assemblage in a wide range of flavors. And if you are concerned about calories, you can use a diet soda.

Now that we've got the basic sauce, let's try it in one of my personal favorites:

Black-Cow Chips

Can of Pringles potato chips
Several packages of chipped beef
Discount or generic root beer
Nondairy creamer

Prepare a root beer roux, as above. Place a stack of Pringles on an empty TV dinner tray and pour roux over them. Wrap each chip in a slice of chipped beef and glue together with roux into a loaf of sorts. Smother one end of the assemblage in French Kiss Sauce (see below) or other topping of your choice.

A conventional TV dinner or fast-food snack takes on a radical new dimension with the addition of a carefully confected sauce like this one.

French Kiss Sauce

French's Mustard
A bag of Hershey's Kisses

Unwrap all Kisses. Eat half, return other half to bag. Place on top of well-watched TV to partially liquefy. Pour half a bottle of mustard into bag and knead the ingredients together. The sauce can be squeezed directly from bag onto your snack.

Remember, good viewing requires good eating. Don't forget the rules you just learned about the basics of snack construction. By properly manipulating these components, your Nutritional Assemblage will exhibit a sublime elegance—and nourish your body as much as the TV programs you view nourish your mind. Eat to view, view to eat!

(For more food tips from Chef Aldo, see "Kitchen Environments," page 52).

PROGRAMMING FACTS

◻ When first conceived the heroine of *The Mary Tyler Moore Show* was to be a divorcee. But CBS nixed it, saying research had shown conclusively that, in sitcoms, American viewers didn't want to see people from New York, people with moustaches or divorcees.

◻ Sponsor Chevrolet insisted that *Bonanza* scriptwriters never direct the characters to "ford" a river—they had to write "cross" instead. Whether they were allowed to "dodge" bullets is unknown.

◻ During the final episode of *M·A·S·H*, more people—125 million—heard Mozart's "Quintet for Clarinet," played by Charles Winchester's Korean band, than in the 200 years since Mozart wrote it.

◻ A few minutes after the last episode of *M·A·S·H* the New York City sewer flow rate suddenly jumped 320 million gallons, the equivalent of 1 million toilets flushing at the same time.

◻ The last commercial in a cluster is the one seen by the most people.

◻ A typical half hour episode of *Cheers* costs $350,000 to make; a typical 30-second McDonald's commercial, $300-500,000. McDonald's spent more on advertising in 1982 than all the House and Senate candidates combined.

◻ Now it can be told: *The Beverly Hillbillies'* house was *not* in Beverly Hills, it was in nearby Bel Air (at 750 Bel Air Drive, to be precise).

◻ The average life of a sitcom in 1960 was 2.26 years. Today it is 0.69 years and shrinking.

◻ The townsfolk of Stanton, Iowa, have painted the 125-foot-high water tower to resemble a giant coffee pot in honor of native daughter Virginia Christine, the Mrs. Olson of Folger's coffee commercial fame.

◻ 70% of all VCR owners have never used its timer.

Environments

Every Room a Viewing Room

Some critics have accused Tubers of taking the "Couch" in our name too literally, of favoring the viewing room model at the expense of other styles of viewing.

True, we *have* preferred to adopt a room of the house, usually the living room, as the exclusive viewing area. The advantages are obvious: you can customize it exclusively for viewing, you needn't lug heavy equipment around the house and, best of all, an aura of proud tradition develops when you view in the same spot year after year surrounded by friends and family.

Yet we admit there are disadvantages. The viewing room tends to get stuffed with people and accessories while other rooms are underutilized, even empty. Couch Potatoes have tried to solve this in a variety of ways:

1. *Move* the viewing room. Might not the kitchen, bathroom, attic or garage be a better place to gather?

2. Make *every* room a viewing room. With video equipment so inexpensive, every-body can afford—by scrimping on rent, food and health care—to buy at least one set for every room, hallway and stairway landing in the house. Keep all sets on constantly, or install infrared switches to activate them at your approach.

3. *Enlarge* the viewing room. If you knock out walls, remove doors and add wide-angle mirrors appropriately, you can make your entire living space one large viewing room. With a projection TV centrally located, nobody will have to miss anything good ever again.

4. *Abolish* the viewing room. One person, one set. Personal freedom and autonomy are now truly possible in a world of inexpensive portables. For some Tubers, the viewing room is an anachronism.

Smart viewers will carefully design their environments to suit their unique needs.

Viewing in the Kitchen

Once considered obsolete by hardcore Tubers, kitchens are making a comeback in the nouvelle Couch Potato cuisine and life-style. And why not? Knock down a few walls and remove unnecessary counters. Add a shag carpet for barefoot comfort, couches, easy chairs and video equipment and your kitchen can be a state-of-the-art viewing room.

Before

After

No more frantic racing from fridge to viewing chair during all-too-short commercial breaks. No more eating tiny meals because that's all that fits into the toaster oven. The appliances you need to keep the food coming are at your fingertips—and they yield unexpected dividends:

■ *Oven.* On cold nights you can turn your oven on low, leave the door open and stick your feet inside. **Warning:** Do not try this with your microwave oven.

■ *Blender.* Good for milkshakes, of course, but you can also use it any time you want to avoid tiresome, noisy chewing. Almost anything can be transformed into its essential state, and it doesn't have to look like unappetizing "astronaut food"—you can make recipes as esthetically pleasing as Chef Aldo's Snickers Pie:

Snickers Pie

Run a couple of graham crackers through the blender and line the bottom of an empty one-serving pot pie tin with crumbs. Blend together several dollops of Cool-Whip and a Snickers bar, then spoon mixture into tin. Chill and serve.

■ *Dishwasher.* Surprisingly, the food-prep potential of the dishwasher remains largely unexploited. After all, this device, designed to spray scalding water within a large enclosed area, is perfect for cooking a wide variety of dishes in unbelievable quantities.

Anything you would normally boil can be run through as many wash cycles as necessary. Nestle several dozen boil-in-the-bag dinners in the dish racks. Most dishwashers can cook carrots and hardboiled eggs in a single Pots & Pans cycle. Cook small vegetables and a variety of pastas in the silverware holders. Or try something fancy like Poached Fish Sticks.

Poached Fish Sticks

Wrap Mrs. Paul's fish sticks individually in aluminum foil, place in dishwasher and run through full wash. Serves one to three hundred people. **Caution:** For best results don't use soap with this or any other recipe. However, a large quantity of Country Time imitation lemonade crystals, used in place of soap, will give the fish a pleasing citrus tang. ("Tang"? Hm, that might be good, too.)

■ *One last warning.* Be careful when mixing food and high-tech electronic equipment. Heed *Cole's Law:* "If you drop your remote control in the mayonnaise, all you'll end up with is Tuner Salad."

Viewing in the Bathroom

During less inhibited times some of the more avant-garde Couch Potato lodges installed bathtubs, sinks and commodes in the main viewing room itself. While this is eminently practical, in these conservative times most of us are too modest for that. We agree with Archie Bunker that "terlets" should be heard and not seen.

Many Tubers, however, experience a profound sense of loneliness and despair behind the bathroom's closed door because they have failed to place a TV set there.

Some cite a fear of electrocution should water get into the TV or TV into the water. Why we can put a TV camera on the moon but cannot make a fully immersible Television is beyond rational comprehension.

On the other hand, many people refuse to put a TV in the bathroom because of a deep, unconscious belief that the people on TV can look out of the box and see them. We have all watched children responding to TV: answering questions Bert and Ernie ask on *Sesame Street;* shouting warnings to Scooby Doo when he's in jeopardy; yelling, "Tackle him, you idiot!" to football players; muttering, "What about the deficit?" during presidential press conferences. Very young children believe they are interacting with

those people who live inside that box.

And that belief never really disappears—it merely gets buried deep in the unconscious. As a result, most people experience a tinge of embarrassment when naked in front of the TV.

This is, of course, ridiculous.

The people on TV *cannot* see us—not unless they actually look directly at the camera. And they vigorously avoid doing so in all but news and kid shows. For these, you can invest in some "modesty curtains," or just go nude and try to make Dan Rather flinch, Jane Pauley blush or Mr. Rogers faint.

Spam on a Rope—A Chef Aldo Handy Hint for Tub Viewing

Trying to eat while luxuriously soaking in the tub can be a big problem. That's why I like Spam on a Rope, an idea sent in by Lori McCracken of Newark, California. Take a whole block of Spam and run it through with a piece of coathanger wire. Bend one end into an L to keep the meat on and the other into an "eye" which can accommodate a piece of rope to hang on a towel rack at mouth level.

Add floatable, watertight squeeze bottles of ketchup and mayo and you have all you need anytime you're in the tub and want to grab a bite of dry meat!

Viewing in the Bedroom

Many people already use the bedroom as their primary viewing room. Some of these Bed Taters do not ever turn their sets off at night, choosing to absorb the benefits of Television subliminally while practicing Closed-Eye Viewing all night long.

Yet, as any fan of *Dallas* knows, there is more to the bedroom than sleeping. We are happy to report that, except for fights about crumbs in bed, bedroom TV viewing can contribute to marital bliss because it is both an aphrodisiac and a contraceptive.

Nothing is sexier than TV programming, especially the commercials. Motivational researchers spend billions of dollars annually to discover the best ways to sell their products by subliminally arousing each and every one of us. Is it any wonder, then, that an evening of TV is the main mode of foreplay for millions of couples worldwide? That Tubers, by virtue of their immeasurable accumulation of sexual energy and uncanny sense of timing, are able to begin and consummate a sexual encounter in the time of one commercial cluster?

Paradoxically, TV is also suitable as an aid to birth control. In some underdeveloped countries (most notably India, where TV is available to the populace only in public, communal viewing areas inconducive to intimate contact) enlightened governments have extended the viewing day into the late evening specifically to help lower the birthrate.

In our own country, couples have used TV schedules in similar, but more sophisticated, fashion. For many years thousands of women used Walter Cronkite's "And that's the way it is. . ." each night as a reminder to take their birth control pill. This may explain the baby boomlet that occurred in the years after Uncle Walter retired.

Similarly, many devout Catholic Tubers mark their "safe days" on the pages of each week's *TV Guide*. Thus they can scan the entire evening's potential pleasures at a single glance.

Finally, there is the Couch Tomatoes' favorite form of contraception: Tuber Libation. That's where you both drink and view so much that you couldn't have sex even if you wanted to.

Viewing in Your Car

Alas, even the most dedicated Tubers have to leave the house at times. That's why it is an absolute necessity to have a good TV set in your car.

Only recently have electronics companies begun to make available TVs manufactured specifically for in-transit viewing. Unfortunately the equipment offered at this writing is less than satisfactory, possibly dangerous. One unit, sold by Nippon Electronics, is an in-dash combination cassette/radio with a tiny TV screen built in. Another company makes a TV set designed to be mounted inside the glove compartment. Both run off the car's battery.

There are two disadvantages to both. You cannot unplug either of them and take them with you—making them susceptible to theft, and leaving you without Television once you arrive at your destination.

Just as bad, there are serious questions about whether it is desirable for drivers to be viewing a screen below and to the right of their normal field of vision. Shifting the eyes from road to TV and back is tiring, potentially unsafe and likely to cause the driver to miss important parts of the TV program.

Instead, we suggest positioning a Sony Watchman or similar portable flat on top of the dashboard so the driver can see the screen's reflection in the windshield superimposed on the car ahead. Almost as good is a set on the rear window ledge to encourage you to use your rearview mirror often (since safety experts say most drivers should check their mirrors more often than they do). Both arrangements have the disadvantage of reversing the TV image, but that shouldn't be a big problem unless you enjoy watching foreign films with subtitles.

Although some anti-TV fanatics will protest about in-transit viewing, Couch Potatoes instinctively know that an in-car TV will make them better drivers. After all, inattention caused by boredom and fatigue is a leading cause of accidents, second only to alcohol abuse. An in-car TV will keep you awake, alert. As the bumper sticker says: "TV doesn't kill people—TV kills *boredom.*" Still, one note of caution: experience has shown that watching *The Dukes of Hazzard, Knight Rider* or anything else with a preponderance of car chases may be slightly disorienting while your car is in motion, so pick your viewing fare with care.

Make Your Viewing Room More "Hospitable"

Why wait to be sick to enjoy the benefits of hospital technology?

Several mail-order companies specialize in these products. A quick glance through their catalogs yields a bonanza of potential viewing accessories: periscopic glasses suitable for viewing while flat on your back, vibrating pillows, heated backrests, adjustable beds, reach extenders, home traction devices, even a "Bedside Johnny" for those times when you're viewing programming without commercials.

Two of the companies are:

Mature Wisdom
Unique Merchandising Mart
Building 28
Hanover, PA 17333

Dr. Leonard's
Health Care Products
65 19th Street
Brooklyn, NY 11232

Requesting a catalog from either company will insure a constant stream of product information from a variety of sources, with no further effort on your part.

Viewing Accessories

■ *Inexpensive Remote Control:* A broom handle with a slot cut in one end can be used to change channels on many TV sets. The other end is suitable for manipulating pushbutton controls and prodding sleeping couchmates who snore.

■ *Wine Pillows:* A tip of the viewing fez to Couch Potato John White of Honolulu for discovering that the bladder from any 4-liter box of Summit wine can make a comfy, sturdy and attractive inflatable pillow. When you finish the wine, grab the plastic spigot and pull the bladder slowly from the box. Rinse it if you want to, but it's not necessary; just open the spigot and inflate with air to desired firmness. The shiny silver plastic foil will give your viewing room a chic high-tech look.

The TV Guide Wall Projector:

A bit of bowling alley technology was borrowed for this handy device that enables the viewer to scan the listings without diverting eyes from the set.

Teleview Reflection Pool

The soothing trickle of water can enhance your viewing pleasure when you assemble a teleview reflection pool and waterfall like this. A few big rocks dug up from the backyard, a kiddies' wading pool and a garden hose attached to an ordinary dust pan are all that you need.

Viewing Environment Maintenance

Naturally, one of the inconveniences of convenience foods is disposing of the leftover packaging. The piles of snack meal refuse that accumulate between station breaks must be dealt with eventually. With this in mind the Couch Potato Lifestyle Laboratories have developed the following maintenance tips to help the viewer sustain his/her video euphoria while keeping the viewing zone tidy.

Before

The Drop Cloth Approach to E-Z Clean-ups

You can add years to the life of your upholstery and carpeting by covering everything with a heavy-duty plastic drop cloth. After the feverish snacking period has subsided, simply bundle up the discards— cans, bottles, wrappers, expendable furniture—and tie up.

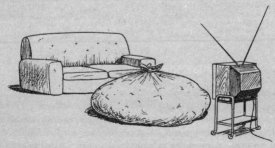

After

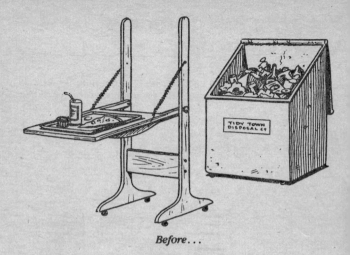

Before...

...In action

Self-clearing TV Tray

Though not yet available commercially, the self-clearing TV tray has proved itself to be an invaluable couchside accoutrement in the upkeep of the snacking area. It can also be used for food fights, passing TV Guides, etc. Anyone with basic junior high school woodworking skills can construct one.

You can improve the ambience of your viewing room and make use of those excess piles of beer cans by carefully balancing them to create this charming grotto effect.

With the E-Z Drain coffee table there's no more running for the clean-up sponge when spills occur. Your coffee table's lovely finish can be easily preserved by providing a drain hole and runoff spout.

Custom TVs

Realizing the need for Televisions that reflect the attitudes and tastes of the specialized viewer, the Couch Potatoes offer the following custom sets:

The Blaster

Like to watch MTV or old reruns of The Monkees *turned up real loud? If so, then this is the setup for you: its hefty speakers really pack a wallop. You'll be able to appreciate your favorite musical programming at entirely new levels. The semiportability of the Blaster will allow the viewer to wheel it down the street for station break dancing.*

The Ruralite

If Green Acres, The Real McCoys, Hee Haw *and* The Beverly Hillbillies *is your idea of really fine programming and you want a TV set that reflects your tastes and enhances your decor, then here's the one for you. The cabinet, crafted from high-grade simulated barnwood, reeks of old-time rustic charm.*

The Futuristocrat

This modular video unit is designed for those who prefer reruns of Star Trek, Battlestar Galactica, Cosmos *and old* Space Patrol *kinescopes. Its sleek advanced styling, complete with audio canopy and fingertip controls, should send any devoted videonaut into orbit.*

The Cinemaddict

Imagine spending days, even weeks on end, basking before your very own altar to the silver screen. Designed with the fan of old movies in mind, this TV combines the elegance of the movie palaces of yesteryear with the comfort and privacy of your own home.

Connoisseur's Choice
This wall-mounted viewing unit is for those who feel that television is truly high art and should be displayed appropriately.

FAMOUS PEOPLE

- Jack Kerouac loved *The Beverly Hillbillies*, sitting a foot from the screen and slugging whiskey from the bottle.

- Sartre has been quoted as saying the only good reason for getting up on Saturday morning is to watch the cartoons on TV.

- Like most Americans, Ronald and Nancy Reagan frequently eat dinner on trays in front of the TV—often the President's favorite meal of macaroni and cheese and coconut cake. One of the President's favorite shows: *Charlie's Angels*. "You know the right people will win no matter how tense it gets," he told an interviewer.

For and About Women Viewers

Women are the most extreme of viewing groups. Teen women watch *less* Television as a group than any other, while women over 55 watch *more* than any other. Why?

One theory postulates that some female hormone impedes the human viewing capacity, since the hormonal levels in women at all ages are almost exactly inversely proportional to their viewing levels. The researchers, noting that women during prime child-bearing age become more aurally oriented, theorize that this may be a natural mechanism to help ensure survival of their babies, since infants communicate much in subtle changes in cries, gurgles and sighs. The female teen phone fixation may be a result of this, the researchers speculate, to the detriment of viewing patterns.

A more plausible explanation holds that stations broadcast female-oriented programming during the day and male-oriented at night and that teen women, owing to the tyranny of compulsory schooling, are deprived of their natural viewing venue. If this theory is true, there's hope of teen women catching up because of two encouraging trends. First, more and more soaps appear on evening TV. And second, industry statistics show that daytime soaps are the programs most often taped on home video recorders.

Why older women watch more than average is discussed in "Lifelong Viewing." While there may be a physiological component, older women probably view more because they have a greater opportunity to view. What's more, they have attained the wisdom to realize that the distractions of their youth are rarely worth leaving the couch for.

The Couch Tomatoes

There has long been confusion about exactly what the Couch Tomatoes are. This is not surprising, because so much of their nature is paradoxical:

■ Strongly sensitive to sexism, they have adopted a name considered by many to be insulting to womanhood.

■ All Couch Tomatoes are

women Tubers, but not all women Tubers are Couch Tomatoes.

■ Originally chartered as a "fetch and adjust" society, they stand accused by some of being a secret, subversive group of "wonder women" working to gain control of couch and TV.

■ While calling themselves Feminists, their stated goal is to return to the viewing habits of traditional womanhood.

This near-schizophrenia has created great confusion, sometimes even within their own ranks. Is this—as some have charged—a purposeful plot to disguise their true goals? Is it mere disorganization and incompetence? Or is it an attempt to emulate the philosophy of their patron saint, Gracie Allen?

Finally, all is revealed. Frankly, the answers may surprise you.

A Short History

As philosophers have pointed out, the present is just the past prerecorded for broadcast at this time. Like the convoluted plot of one of their favorite soaps, to understand what is happening with the Couch Tomatoes today you must first know what occurred in previous episodes.

Sheepish Revelations: It is a source of organizational embarrassment that the Couch Tomatoes, a club for women, was founded by men. This was decades ago when, on Television at least, "men were men and women were kitchen appliances," as one historian put it. Women on TV—from June Cleaver through hundreds of commercial characters to Aunt Bea—taught us all that women should be cleaners of sinks, clothes, floors, dishes and toilet bowls; preparers of food; and fulfillers of men's wishes. The Couch Tomatoes were created to conform to that idyllic image. At the time, the women were willing to serve. This arrangment worked for several years—not that women didn't mind missing shows to make sandwiches or run down to the store for more beer, but on the whole they were reasonably content. So, of course, were the men.

Paradise Lost: In the late sixties and early seventies, TV society changed. Gradually we saw women on the screen living their own lives, on shows like *Here's Lucy, Julia, That Girl, The Mary Tyler Moore Show* and *Maude*. These winds of change blew through the hermetically sealed lodges of the Couch Potatoes. Couch Tomatoes, who for years had uncomplainingly cooked, changed channels and made emergency MalloCup runs, gradually grew aware of their suppressed resentment. In lodge after lodge, the spontaneous female battle cry was heard: "Get it yourself, asshole!"

The men of the couch, although surprised by these outbursts, attributed them to periodic hormonal changes and assumed the furor would all blow over. It didn't. The women began gathering together in kitchens around the country, viewing what *they* wanted to watch instead of going along with the men's preferences, and ignoring the pleas from the main viewing rooms for more beer and for tuning assistance.

The women discovered that they were just as capable as the men when it came to the fine arts of indolence and prolonged viewing. But they were still second-class citizens in the main viewing rooms, and this made them mad.

The Equal Rights to the Couch movement had begun.

Tomatoes Ripe for Change: In the mid-seventies the organization came within an antenna's-width of dividing. Some

lodges actually applied for a spot on *Divorce Court* and began the painful task of splitting their video equipment into two equal parts.

Yet somehow a flicker of compromise, fair play and trust survived, which, combined with inertia, carried the day. The Couch Potatoes opened full membership to women, and *General Hospital* became acceptable viewing fare in most lodges. There was talk of phasing out the Tomato organization, but the women decided instead to reorganize it within the Couch Potato fold with a new mission: to safeguard women's viewing interests and act as a forum for communication of important issues, like who is doing what to whom on *Days of Our Lives*. "Tomato," once considered a pejorative term, was retained as a symbol of female pride in the struggle that won them their viewing rights— and because of a reluctance to buy new stationery.

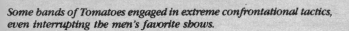

Some bands of Tomatoes engaged in extreme confrontational tactics, even interrupting the men's favorite shows.

Beauty Tips for the Couch Tomato

Not only can Television make a woman smart, it can make her beautiful, too. Radiation from the screen and the Couch Tomato lifestyle bring out the natural pallid skin tones, the dark sunken eyes, the Reubenesque, pear-shaped weight distribution so irresistible to the male Tuber.

The best way to achieve this look is, of course, the natural way: long hours of viewing in a darkened room, plenty of carbohydrates and a cushy chair. But sometimes a woman wants to accentuate (and make up for the deficiencies of) what nature and Grant Tinker have given her.

Unfortunately, most cosmetics are designed to look good in sunlight and artificial lighting, not in the warm glow of the Electronic Hearth. Furthermore, most come in unnatural reds and tans which give the impression that the wearer has been out in deadly, carcinogenic sunlight all day—not an image that will inspire thoughts of romance.

Worse, the compatible partners Couch Tomatoes are trying to attract generally have their eyes glued elsewhere. The secret is to avoid competing with the TV. Instead a Tomato must learn to work *with* the TV to make her love connection.

Let's approach the technique one step at a time:

Complexion:

A good chemical supplier will be able to supply you with the phosphors TV manufacturers put inside picture tubes to glow when light strikes them. If you mix the phosphors with a very pale facial powder and apply it to your skin you will literally glow in the light of the TV. Use a soft eyebrow pencil to paint some subtle horizontal "scan lines" across your face, and your couch mate will stare at you for hours.

Eyes: All's fair in love, even using subliminal network symbols to catch the eye of your favorite Tuber. Try making up your eyes to resemble the CBS logo or paint the NBC Peacock on your eyelids. You will become more exciting in his eyes as he subconsciously remembers all the good times he's had with his favorite networks. A generous application of eye makeup effectively cuts down video glare during those long hours of all-night reruns and movies.

From this

to THIS!

Lips: Most Couch Tomatoes avoid wearing lipstick. It has the tendency to smear and foul the taste of favorite snack foods like corny dogs, burritos and pickles. If you really want a little color in your lips, eat a cherry-flavored Popsicle every half hour or so.

Perfume: Many Couch Tomatoes have been wearing the wrong perfume for the wrong reason: they thought Chanel No. 5 was French for "channel 5." Better to use a little psychology in your scent selection. What is most attractive to the male Tuber? (1) TV and (2) food.

So it's logical that you should smell like one or the other. Experiment with favorite foods that have distinctive aromas. Rub a little Hershey's syrup behind each ear. Or substitute that tasty red powder left over in the bottom of the Bar-B-Q chips bag for your usual blusher (better to use Cremora nondairy creamer because the color is more natural).

Splurge and buy yourself a scent like *L'Air de Tube*, designed to bring on a feeling of nostalgia by smelling like the ozone given off by antique Dumonts and RCAs.

A Beautiful Body: Couch Tomatoes, like many women, are unduly sensitive about their weight. Most are concerned either that they do not weigh enough or that the bulk they carry around with them is in the wrong places. "Whenever I try to gain weight below the waist, it always congregates in the bust area," is a common complaint.

The ideal, of course, is a healthy bottom-heavy pear shape that gives extra padding for prolonged sitting and provides ballast so you can stay seated on the Couch even when asleep or otherwise unconscious.

How can you gain enough weight in the right places? Try the Couch Tomato Fad Diet, based on immutable laws of physics and forty years of research by independent industry-sponsored test labs. The premise is simple: the heavier the food, the lower on the body the resulting fat will collect. Since the body is 92% water, foods will float at a level consistent with their relative weight.

The fat will go straight to your bottom if you eat only dense, heavy foods. If you are not sure which foods qualify, fill your bathtub with water and try floating them. Foods that sink to the bottom, you'll find, will seek the same level in your body. Soon you'll be able to put your weight problems behind you.

Couch Tomato Hairstyles

It's amazing what you can come up with, using a little imagination and several cans of hairspray. You'll be sure to improve your reception at any gala viewing event with these coifs.

The Cathode Caprice
Present your own features in this appropriate frame by teasing, spraying and setting to the desired shape.

The Mostest *(inspired by Hostess)*
Here the hair is pulled up and away from the ears, then molded to a flared crown to suggest the famous cupcake (squiggle on top may be created with any aerosol whipped topping).

Satellite Delight
Here's an inspired creation that will transform any lady into an enticing satellite dish. Hair is swept up to the forelock area, where it is formed into the familar dish shape.

The Vertical Hold
This lovely bouffant is shaped while lounging on the couch after the hair is doused with liberal amounts of spray.

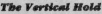

La Femme d'Antenne
Hair is molded up from ear to ear to create the proper pitch at the ornamented peak.

Couch Tomato Fashions: How Good Viewing Can Transform You Into a Good Looker

While giant fuzzy slippers, hair rollers and a well-worn bathrobe will never go out of style in the viewing room, some ladies of the couch like to blaze their own fashion trails for those special situations. Look to your favorite characters for inspiration:

Wilma

Questing a little fire in your life? Inspired by a popular show from the Bronze Age of Television, the soft rugged-cut fleece will help you make fashion prehistory among your fellow troglodyte viewers.

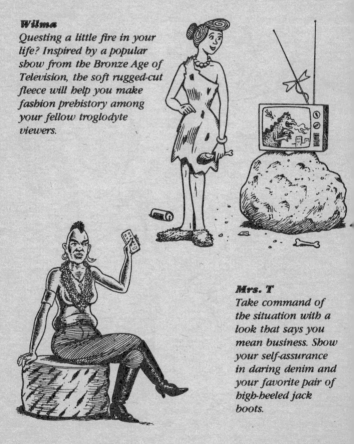

Mrs. T

Take command of the situation with a look that says you mean business. Show your self-assurance in daring denim and your favorite pair of high-heeled jack boots.

Jeannie
You can make your man's dream of Jeannie come true when you suddenly appear before his TV set wearing this classically elegant outfit. Weave magic powers over your "master" when you join him for 1001 nights of rerun fun.

Bird Song
In this outfit with its one-size-fits-all Expandex comfort and stain-resistant bib, you don't have to eat like a bird when perched on the couch.

Arts and Crafts for the Couch Tomato

For years women have combined TV viewing with activities that beautify themselves, their homes and their loved ones. For some reason many women seem incapable of sitting still without something to keep their hands busy: a clothes iron, unsorted socks, a manicure set, an embroidery hoop or knitting needles. While their eyes remain transfixed by the set, their hands fly in furious motion.

While some see this as a serious sex-linked genetic defect, we say, "Don't mess with it." This condition, after all, has resulted in millions of handknit sweaters and socks, in thousands of handcrafted imitation-leather *TV Guide* covers, in more afghans in America than in all Afghanistan.

While Couch Tomatoes are less prone to this condition than most women, many do apparently enjoy this "chewing gum for the hands." They complain, though, that few crafts result in objects expressive of, and useful to, the Prolonged Viewing lifestyle, and even fewer that use the large quantities of raw materials available to them as by-products of it. We offer some suggestions to rectify this:

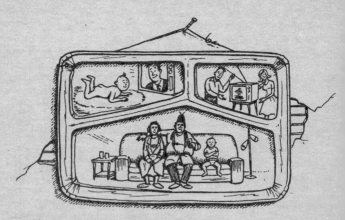

TV Dinner Picture Frame: Your friends will think you "tray" chic" when you present them with photos in this high-tech picture frame. Best of all, you don't even have to leave the couch to get paste if you put photos in place before the leftover gravy congeals.

Simulated Imitation-Leather *TV Guide* Cover:

While some women have actually invested in the tools and materials necessary to make a permanent imitation-leather *TV Guide* cover, it is possible to achieve the same effect by attaching plastic contact paper to the cover of each issue. Stick with the classic leather look, or go for variety: wood grain one week, a bright pastel the next, imitation brick the week after.

TV Guide TV Duster/Waterless Houseplant/Christmas Tree:

Overlap pages torn out of *TV Guide* as pictured and roll up. Secure resulting tube with tape or rubber band. With scissors make four cuts lengthwise, two-thirds of the way to the bottom. Pull up on innermost "leaves" and watch your "never-needs-watering" plant grow!

Beer Pop-Top Chains/Curtains/Room Dividers:

Many states have outlawed cans with removable pop-tops—if yours has not, count your blessings and save your pop-tops to hook into chains. Some lodges in states with these repressive laws have concocted elaborate pop-top smuggling rings, but inevitably pop-tops will become a thing of the past everywhere, so this is your chance to own a valuable future antique. Multiple chains can be hung side by side to make glimmering curtains and room dividers, brilliantly reflecting the colors of your TV screen. Beautiful, and they cure curtain-climbing cats in a hurry, too!

Garbage Bag Hassocks:

Hefty heavy-duty garbage bags, with their bold graphics and multi-ply construction, are too good to merely throw away. They make great hassocks when filled, and you can further decorate them, if you wish. *Hint:* Your hassock will smell better if you do not use biodegradable stuffing (banana peels, bread crusts, etc.)—instead, use shredded styro cups, paper, cellophane and anything with a shelflife of a year or more. Twinkies, Ding-Dongs and Hostess Cupcakes do just fine.

Wonder Bread Play Dough:

Fresh white bread can be dampened and molded. Pop in toaster oven set for low heat and it will harden more or less permanently. Color with artificial food dyes before molding, or paint after hardening. One loaf, sans crusts, makes a fist-size lump of "clay."

Knitting and Crocheting: No longer do you have to put up with the flying-duck and jumping-fish designs (so ubiquitous in craft magazines) that are antithetical to the Tuber lifestyle. Try this afghan design in your choice of colors. If you like it, the pattern can be easily adapted to couch pillows, hand-hooked rugs, sweaters, rabbit earmuffs and TV dinner cosies.

TV Afghan

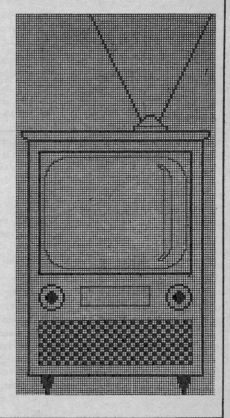

Size: 64 × 42 inches
4 stitches = 1 inch
4 rows = 1 inch
Use #11 29-inch circular needle and worsted-weight yarn (grease-resistant washable acrylic is best). Cast on 168 stitches. Knit one row, purl one row for 11 inches. Continuing in pattern, knit 37 stitches, knit first row of chart, knit 36 stitches, color A.

Follow chart, keeping 41 stitches to each side in color A.

Continuing pattern, follow chart until end. Knit one, purl one row for 11 inches, color A. Bind off.

An Indian-head test pattern quilt can be a good project for a video quilting bee.

Craft Designs From Your TV: Free yourself forever from the tyranny of insipid craft magazines and their incessant grid patterns. All you need is a video player with freeze-frame function and some transparent graph paper. Tracing paper is all right, but clear plastic works better and lasts longer.

Insert your favorite tape or disc, fast-forward to your favorite image and hit the freeze-frame button. Attach graph paper over TV screen. Now when you knit, crochet or hook a rug you can use the image on the screen as if it were a pattern from a magazine. Your Ralph Kramden sweater, your Tom Magnum afghan, your Chase Gioberti pillow and your T. J. Hooker rug will make you the envy of your sewing-and-viewing circle!

Telecastrology

by Madame Quasar Dumont

Madame Quasar Dumont is a Seer in a world of viewers, the premiere Couch Potato psychic guide and spirit interpreter. She is the originator of Kukla Phren-Ology, the analysis of puppet personality by head shape, and Sidekick Healing, achieving wellness by emulating Tonto, Ed McMahon, Illya Kuryakin, Ed Norton, and other second bananas. In a past life she foretold the existence of Television and "applied for a Cosmic Channel Change," as she puts it, so she could be here to guide us through the powerful new medium. She is aided by her spirit guides George, Marion and Neal-the-dog.

Hello, seekers. Do you ever find yourself saying, "There must be more to Television than what we can see?" Has the fourth chakra in your spine ever tingled with the feeling that you've seen this show before? Do you know what's going to happen days before your *TV Guide* arrives in the mail? Do you find that watching *The $25,000 Pyramid* helps your houseplants grow, increases your powers of concentration and sharpens your razor blades? Do you ever have the feeling your TV is trying to tell you something?

You may have hidden psychic powers. Many Tubers just like you have exhibited telegenic and kinescopic powers, déjà view experiences and remarkable ghost image interpretations. This is not an area to be dealt with frivolously—look what happened in *Poltergeist,* after all, when a Naïve tapped into the occult powers of Television— but a level-headed, stable, *normal* Tuber like yourself will find the power within to wrestle the TV-revealed cosmic forces of the universe and throw them for a fall. While most mystics have to settle for a mere Third Eye, a Potato has thousands. That's why I sense that *you* are spiritually ready to use the powerful techniques I am about to reveal.

TV Horoscope

Too many Seekers are suckers. Perhaps they need to watch PBS more often to exercise their dormant critical facilities.

Take astrology...please! Maybe the theory made sense in the past when radiation from distant stars was the primary source of cosmic energy on this planet. But anybody with even half an Earth Sign's worth of common sense would realize how insignificant this energy has become compared to the strong, omni-present Television signals which radiate through us from all directions. Astrology is dead—the Truly Illuminated now chart their futures with *Tele-castrology*.

Narrowcasting Your Chart: First of all, the Telecastrologer must know what was being broadcast in your birth place at the exact moment you were born. If you were born after 1953, try finding old *TV Guides*. Otherwise, check the news-paper file in your local library or contact the TV stations directly to see if they've still got their old broadcast logs filed away somewhere. The relative strength of each TV signal deter-mines its dominance on the chart.

Once the broadcast signals are charted in descending strength, the telecastrologer is ready to examine each sign and see how it interacts with the others. Certain configurations of broad-cast towers create what I call "interference patterns." For instance, two towers at a 180° angle are said to be in *opposition,* and the net result is a reduced effectiveness for each. Other arrays can accentuate each influence—three towers in a *trine,* or rough equilateral triangle, for example.

Let's suppose you were born on Wednesday, October 3, 1968 at 8:21 p.m. in San Francisco's St. Gregory Hospital. Channels 7 and 2 are in *conjunction,* boosting their influence. Chan-nels 9 and 44 are in *opposition,* diminishing their influence. Here are the stations in order of dominance:

7 *The Flying Nun* (ABC): A rare Double Air sign, since it is both a comedy (levity=levitation) and about flying, yet its potent influence is slightly mitigated since the birth took place in the last half of the show (*descendency*). Still, it is the dominant sign in this configuration.

A person born under the Flying Nun tends to be good-humored, of catholic tastes, spiritual, high-spirited, imprac-tical, sexually repressed, light-headed, to have difficulty in keeping feet on the ground, and an affinity with penguins.

2 *I Spy* (indepen-dent station, rerun): A Fire Sign, like all cop and spy shows, in  ascendency. People born dur-ing reruns are prone to déjà view experiences.

Characteristics: Observant, cool-headed, patriotic, good at tennis, glib, fond of travel, voyeuristic; has a tendency to see things in terms of black and white.

5 *Hawaii Five-O* (CBS): Fire sign, in ascendency. Characteristics: Law-abiding, active, occasionally violent, insular, tendency to drive too fast and wear funny shirts.

4 *Daniel Boone* (NBC): Earth Sign, in descendency. Characteristics: basic common sense, leadership, attuned to nature, not very smart, poor grooming, likes to wear pieces of dead animals on body.

9 *Pete Seeger* (PBS): Water Sign, as are all musical and variety shows, in descendency.

Characteristics: political independence, musical, compassionate, activist, enjoys coercing strangers into singing chorus after chorus of *If I Had a Hammer*.

44 *Hazel* (independent station, rerun): Air Sign, in descendency.

Characteristics: Nosy, unambitious, earthy good sense, kindhearted, uneducated, good-intentioned, meddling, does windows.

Larry, Moe and Kirlian Photography

Every living thing has a soul or aura, a life essence that surrounds it. This strangely colored glowing mist was once visible only to certain psychic specialists or through a complicated photographic process involving electricity and expensive equipment. But now you don't really need expensive equipment or the services of a powerful spirit guide, because an even more powerful medium—Television—awaits you in your living room *right now* to help you see the unseeable.

Television is more perceptive than we mortals. It sees all, records all—even the auras of the people on the screen. What we call Ghost Images are literally that: the spiritual essence of everyone who has ever been on Television, seeking us through Channel One.

Most viewers foolishly try to tune out Ghost Images, but the illuminated Tuber will try to tune them *in.* What better way to prove to the doubters the existence of the Soul?

If you have trouble seeing Ghost Images, try disconnecting your antenna. Or move into a neighborhood with skyscrapers nearby, since tall buildings seem to attract spirits and other manifestations of the Other World.

Automatic Viewing

Automatic Viewing superficially resembles the Couch Potato technique of Simulviewing. Practitioners of both watch many screens tuned to different channels. However, twenty or more sets

are required for Automatic Viewing—enough to overwhelm all worldly senses. And the Automatic Viewer tries *not* to fixate on Material World considerations like plot, characterization and dialogue.

First, adjust all screens to the same brightness, and set the volume so that your viewing space is filled with indistinguishable murmuring. Then sit back, relax and open yourself to the Cosmic Influences. Try gently chanting a TV mantra (Yabba-Dabba-Doo is my favorite) to quiet the conscious part of your mind. If that doesn't do the trick, drink four or five beers and try again. Actively refrain from paying attention to any one screen or soundtrack; instead, try to tune in all of them at once.

Long hours may pass before certain words, phrases and images begin to command your attention, the way you hear your name spoken across a crowded, noisy room. Stay detached and relaxed, but watch and listen. Eventually you will become conscious of a pattern in the fragments that compel your attention. This is a message from beyond our world: perhaps a prediction of the future; possibly wise counsel from the spirits who permeate the airwaves; maybe even a missive from a beloved deceased couchmate or favorite canceled sitcom character.

If you have only one TV set available but still want to tune into the Cosmos, you can get something of the same effect by taping down your channel-scan button (I use Mystic tape, of course) so channel after channel passes continuously in quick succession.

Or, if you have the courage, try the Crystal Snow Ball method.

The Crystal Snow Ball

Seers in the old days had crystal balls to help focus their psychic energy. I use the "snow" on off-channels to achieve the same effect. Adjust the set as bright as you can and turn up the white noise soundtrack loud enough to screen out all distractions like street noises, the telephone and family members. Sit a foot or two away in a relaxed but alert state of mind. With perseverance you may begin to see and hear cryptic but meaningful patterns and messages in the seemingly random dots and noises. Be careful, though: my cousin Philco Dumont suddenly disappeared when his wife abruptly tuned to *The Twilight Zone* in mid-seance.

TV AROUND THE WORLD _____

☐ The United States contains more than one-third of the world's supply of TVs, averaging more than two sets per household.

☐ In high demand in the Russian and Polish black markets are VCR tapes of forbidden American movies and porn.

☐ TV goes dark every Monday night by brutal government fiat in Hungary.

☐ Among shows imported by the Chinese in their first use of American programming: *Muggable Mary: Street Cop, Quarterback Princess,* four Dr. Seuss specials, selected football games (broadcast with lengthy explanations in Chinese before, during and after the games) and commercials—five minutes per hour.

☐ In India, VCRs are so popular (and necessary since there is only one, mostly educational, channel in the country) that groups of up to 50 will pool their meager resources to jointly buy one.

☐ By popular demand Israeli programmers were forced to reschedule *Wonder Woman* later on Saturday so devout Jews observing the Sabbath would have time to get home from synagogues to watch it.

☐ Soap operas in Brazil actually incorporate commercials into the plot, for a special fee: A heroine pointedly drinks Tang; her maid mows the lawn while proclaiming the virtues of the mower. Later she goes to a doctor who enthusiastically recommends a sponsor's over-the-counter cure-all.

☐ Almost all countries have soaps, often with cultural twists. Recently, on Egypt's *The Rusty Statue,* a wife cleverly dealt with her husband's extramarital affair by befriending the other woman and then encouraging the husband to take her on as a second wife, creating a united front against the hapless man.

◻ The Japanese view the most TV per capita, averaging a daily 8 hours 14 minutes per household in the Tokyo area—over an hour more than Americans. And when a poll asked which of the following they would keep if they had to give up all but one— TV, newspapers, telephone, automobile or refrigerator—a gratifying 31% of the Japanese chose TV, as opposed to a disappointing 3% of Americans.

◻ In certain emerging African countries *I Love Lucy* is so popular that the name Lucy rivals traditional tribal names for girls.

A View From Across the Sea

Are You Dependent on Television?

1. On the average, do you watch TV 3 hours a day?

2. You have only one TV and that broke. Are you going to look here, there and everywhere to see who can lend you one?

3. You didn't go to work because of a small toothache. Are you going to spend all morning watching TV?

4. Your girlfriend has personal problems and is begging you to spend an evening with her. Before you accept, are you going to check what's on TV that night?

5. Do you have the habit of changing the channel every few minutes so you don't miss anything?

6. All day long you've looked forward to a certain program, but you can't watch it because your husband has invited friends for a card party. Are you going to be mad?

7. Do you remember most of the Economic Propaganda (commercials) that you hear?

8. The minute you buy the newspaper, do you open it to the TV listings?

9. Do you remember in detail how Olivia Mlakar was dressed in the last episode of Kviskoteki?

10. Can you name the main characters in the serial The Hospital at the Edge of the City?

—A self-diagnostic poll from Yugoslavian women's magazine *Svijet* ("The World"), April 1983. (Translated by Davorka James)

TV: Don't Leave Home Without It

Even the most TV-marinated Couch Potato cannot avoid occasional attacks of wanderlust, especially after watching multiple episodes of travel shows like *The Love Boat*, *Route 66* or *The Fugitive*. Before packing, though, take some time to lean back and think it over. Is this trip necessary?

If you decide to defy the laws of inertia and make that trip, take special care with your advance preparations. Besides buying a second portable TV set and plenty of emergency backup batteries, check to see that the motels, friends and family you intend to visit have acceptable video equipment and an adequate number of channels. Avoid "set lag"—sudden, panicked disorientation caused by unfamiliar TV schedules—by obtaining copies of *TV Guide* for the areas you intend to visit and consulting them frequently while traveling.

Viewing in Transit

Whoever first said "getting there is half the fun" wasn't a Couch Potato. Viewing on long-distance trips is about as much fun as having your favorite show pre-empted by a Billy Graham special.

First of all, forget about flying, unless you consider an in-flight movie an adequate

A transient Tuber using the compact "Jet Set" (concealed here in an attache case) openly defies aeronautical regulations against in-flight TV viewing.

replacement for true viewing. Petty FAA regulations forbid the use of portable TV sets on any airline in this country merely because they might jam navigation and communication devices in the cockpit.

While AmTrak and the bus lines allow you to view as long as you hold your equipment on your lap and use an earphone, there's a catch: reception in aluminum and stainless steel vehicles is terrible in the best of areas and nonexistent else-where. That means having to carry a portable VCR in your lap, too—an arrangement which, during long trips, could result in chronically cold feet or even gangrene.

Clearly, traveling in a private vehicle is the best of several dismal choices. Even so, there are vast wastelands in this supposedly civilized country that are completely devoid of TV signals and other areas that receive only one or two channels—near-starvation for those of us accustomed to a video feast.

Roughing It

For some Tubers it only takes one episode too many of *Daniel Boone, Wild Kingdom* or a *National Geographic* special to start them dreaming of a Watch-man in a forest glade and TV dinners over an open fire.

Fortunately, most never get past the dreaming stage. The terrors of the wild (dangerous animals, plague-bearing vampiric insects, deadly lightning, car-cinogenic sunlight, rabid chip-munks, quicksand, falling rocks and tree limbs, flash floods, psychopathic hermit woodsmen, life-threatening temperature ex-tremes, poisonous reptiles, carnivorous plants, forest fires, outlaw motorcycle gangs, poison oak and ivy, ax accidents, polluted water supplies, acid rain, earthquakes, hurricanes, and renegade Indians) are bad enough, but all pale against the damnably bad Television recep-tion in nearly all wilderness areas.

A survey of five popular Na-tional Parks yielded dismal news for TV aficionados: little or no TV in all but one.

■ *Yellowstone Park* may be old, but it is less than faithful to us Tubers. No TVs in any of the park's hotels, no reception anywhere in the park except at the extreme north end near Mammoth Hot Springs where you can pick up three snowy channels from Billings and Idaho Falls. Best way to see the park is to pick up the *Yellowstone Highlights* home videocassette, narrated by Telly Salavas, at one of the park stores. Even better, take along a good supply of *Yogi Bear* tapes.

Back-to-nature viewing is invigorating, but it's not always worth the hardships.

It's not impossible to coerce the dedicated Tuber into enjoying the great outdoors.

■ Forget *Yosemite,* Sam: no TV reception. Try nearby Lake Tahoe instead, where you can videotape your loved ones with wax figures of Ben, Adam, Hoss and Little Joe Cartwright at the Ponderosa Ranch Gift Shop.

■ If you're hoping to watch *Wally Gator* cartoons in the swampy *Everglades,* think again—it's not available on snowy channel 6 out of Miami. The in-park hotel's new antenna picks up a few other Miami channels (4, 7 and 12), but you'll have to pay plenty for a deluxe suite or watch in black-and-white, and none of these channels carry Wally, either.

■ Visit the *Grand Canyon* and you'll get nothing but a deep depression: no TV reception. But if you're in the area anyway visit the RV/trailer theme park with a *Flintstones*/Bedrock motif at the junction of highways 64 and 180. Yabba-dabba-doo!

■ Of the five surveyed, only *Shenandoah Park* in Virginia is a bluelight beacon of hope to Couch Potatoes. You can pick up eight or nine channels from Richmond and Washington, D.C., anywhere in the park. But the hotel is a letdown: one communal TV in the lobby, none in the rooms.

It is scandalous that taxpaying TV viewers are so discriminated against in our wilderness park system. Where is James Watt when we need him?

For now, back-to-nature Couch Potatoes would best invest in one of those gigantic three-gallons-to-the-mile recreational vehicles advertised on late-night TV. Convert it into a viewing room on wheels and drive it onto that concrete camping space. Once you get your portable generator started up and the VCRs humming, you won't even have to go outside: just camp yourself into an easy chair, open a beer and settle back. Ah, nature!

Good viewing etiquette—and your personal safety—require turning your TV's sound up louder than usual, day and night. Not only will this keep away bears and rabid chipmunks, but it will give your less-privileged neighbors in tents the chance to be entertained by your collection of rare *Flying Nun* episodes. Best of all, the reassuring reverberations from your set and generator will drown out the jarring overnight din of crickets, birds and wind in the trees, so you and the rest of the camp can dream restful dreams of Yogi Bear and Woodsy Owl in the flickering glow of your Sony Trinitron.

Don't let lack of funds halt your wanderlust. A small battery-operated portable can be an indispensable companion for the indigent traveler.

Stay-at-Home Alternatives to Camping Out

◼ Park your TV-outfitted RV in your driveway and "camp" there for the adventure of "getting away from it all" combined with the nearby comforts of home. Or even better, arrange with the manager of your local 7-11 store to let you camp in the parking lot so snacks and beverages will always be readily available.

◼ Ask your friends to make a copy of home videos of their travels. Any competent video studio can easily superimpose you and your family onto the tapes for a fraction of the effort and expense of taking the vacation yourselves!

Regional TV Folklore

Thanks in large part to Television's influence, regional differences are rapidly disappearing in the United States. And good riddance, we say. No longer does the unwary traveler have to worry about not being able to understand the gas station attendant's directions or about being served something strange in a middle-of-nowhere greasy spoon: people everywhere are talking more and more like Tom Brokaw and Johnny Carson, and each of the 140 nationally advertised Big Macs served every second worldwide is exactly the same no matter where you get it.

But change moves faster in some places than others. Some one-channel towns, resisting TV's tendency to wipe out local traditions, have incorporated the Tube into their community life. The viewing party has supplanted the quilting bee, and the video rental outlet has replaced the feed store as the place to swap a few lies with friends and neighbors. Television has even been incorporated into the folklore and superstitions passed from generation to generation, according to Couch Potato anthropologist Lee K. Scull, who collected these examples in Appalachia, the Deep South and Toledo, Ohio:

◼ It's bad luck to watch channel 13 on Friday.

◼ A viewing dog will not bite.

◼ If, on TV reruns, you see somebody who has died, you must whistle the *Topper* theme three times at midnight during the next full moon or your TV set will henceforth have ghost images.

◼ You can turn bad fortunes to good by carrying a pair of lucky rabbit ears.

■ No horse should have two masters; no TV should have two remote channel changers.

■ CBS is owned by devil worshipers; the letters stand for "Called By Satan." One popular TV preacher is the Antichrist and will reveal himself when he stars in a show called *The 666 Club*.

■ In order to predict what is going to be on TV a week in advance, the *TV Guide* employs a stable of psychics even larger than that of the *National Enquirer*.

■ A large-screen TV playing in the middle of your cornfield is the best scarecrow.

■ Don't buy a Sony TV because the Japanese, still angry over losing World War II, have installed small but deadly bombs inside. Someday all Japanese TVs will simultaneously explode on a signal broadcast from submarines off America's coasts.

The Ultimate Couch Potato Tour

Qualified Tubers are invited to join us on the Ultimate Couch Potato Tour, a cross-country pilgrimage in comfortable TV-equipped RVs to the hometowns of our favorite TV characters.

We'll meet for a marathon Viewing at the Museum of Broadcasting in New York City and meander our way to Hollywood through thirty-five years of Television's greatest sites and sights. From Mayfield to Mayberry, from Hooterville to Doodyville, from Central City all the way to Fernwood, Ohio, we'll go home again to the familiar houses, stores, schools and city streets we have wandered through in episode after episode of our favorite shows.

The traveling viewing rooms—actually tractor trailer trucks customized with dozens of TV sets, couches and all the comforts of home viewing modules—will feature undistracted, nonglare viewing because there will be no windows. Instead, TV cameras mounted on top of the trucks will allow us to see everything on closed-circuit monitors without leaving the comforts of the couch!

While a trip like this won't be cheap, you'll rerun it in your memory for years to come. And complete, unedited videocassettes of the entire trip will be available. Watch for further information in late-night commercials on small local TV stations.

Typical Day's Schedule

Day One: New York Metropolitan Area

1. View at the Museum of Broadcasting, Manhattan.

2. Breakfast with Felix Unger and Oscar Madison at their apartment on Park Avenue (*The Odd Couple*).

3. Morning snack with Cissy and Jody (but, alas, not Buffy) at 600 East 32nd Street (*Family Affair*).

4. A cup of Maxwell House with Danny and Kathy Williams in their East 50th Street apartment (*Make Room for Daddy*).

5. Lunch: bagels and lox with the Goldbergs in the Bronx (*The Goldbergs*).

6. Knock down a few afternoon drinks at *Archie's Place* in Queens.

7. Follow Ralph Kramden's bus home to Brooklyn for dinner with him, Alice and the Nortons (*The Honeymooners*).

8. Evening entertainment: dance the minuet with Kathy in Brooklyn Heights and see if a hot dog still makes her identical cousin Patty lose control (*The Patty Duke Show*).

9. Spend the night parked in front of Rob and Laura Petrie's New Rochelle suburban digs (*Dick Van Dyke Show*). While we rest, Hazel the maid will drive in from Hydsberg, New York, to freshen up each viewing area.

Other Itinerary Highlights:

- Mayfield *(Leave It to Beaver)*
- Hilldale *(Ozzie and Harriet, The Donna Reed Show)*
- Hillsdale *(Dennis the Menace)*
- Springfield *(Father Knows Best)*
- Central City *(Dobie Gillis)*
- Jefferson City *(Mr. Peepers)*
- Bryant Park *(My Three Sons)*
- Washington, D.C. *(Get Smart, The Farmer's Daughter)*
- Mayberry, NC *(Andy Griffith)*
- Cocoa Beach, FL *(I Dream of Jeannie)*
- Chicago *(Bob Newhart)*
- Madison *(Our Miss Brooks)*
- Fernwood, OH *(Mary Hartman)*
- Cincinnati *(WKRP)*
- Minneapolis *(The Mary Tyler Moore Show)*
- Milwaukee *(Happy Days, Laverne and Shirley)*
- Dallas
- Doodyville, TX *(Howdy Doody)*
- Grover City *(Sky King)*
- North Fork, NM *(The Rifleman)*
- Ojai, CA *(Bionic Woman)*
- San Pueblo, CA *(Partridge Family)*
- Beverly Hills *(Bachelor Father, Beverly Hillbillies, Burns & Allen)*
- Camp Henderson, CA *(Gomer Pyle)*
- Los Angeles *(Life of Riley, CHIPS, et al.)*
- Bedrock ruins archeological dig *(Flintstones)*

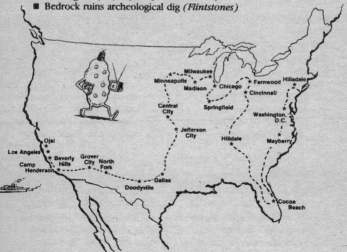

My Sony Lies Over the Ocean: Traveling Abroad

Only the extremely brave—or foolhardy—should travel abroad. All the difficulties of domestic travel exist, multiplied tenfold. TV is different over there, profoundly different: in language, in types of programming, in voltage, even in technology, so that in many countries your video equipment will be useless—if it even survives the journey.

The only good news is that most quality hotels have TVs, just like in the United States. Less easily solved are the programming and language difficulties. We've heard reports of strange, incoherent quiz shows, convoluted soap operas and incomprehensible discussion shows—from travelers who understood the language! For the rest of us, TV becomes a purely visual medium.

Not to say you can't see American TV shows. Most countries import our best: *Colombo, Dallas, The A-Team, Laverne and Shirley.* Unfortunately they also dub them. But most of us have seen the episodes often enough to know what Lucy and Desi are bickering about even if they're talking Greek, Spanish, Japanese or Hindi.

More chilling is the number of so-called civilized countries that practice political persecution of TV viewers. Censorship, repression and neglect keep billions from seeing the quality of TV fare we Americans take for granted. Consider these tip-of-the-iceberg examples:

■ In Iceland, TV broadcasting is *prohibited by law* for a full 79 days a year. The population, as a result, is prone to vice and antisocial behavior: alcoholism and suicide rates are high and, alarmingly, there are more bookstores per capita than in any other country.

■ *I Love Lucy* has been banned in certain Arabic countries because Lucy "dominates" Desi.

■ In Canada, the Domestic Content Law limits the amount of non-Canadian programming. (If you have ever seen Canadian programming, you can understand why certain elements in the country want to secede.) We expect better from the country that gave us Lorne Greene, Dan Ackroyd, Raymond Burr.

William Shatner, Jay (Tonto) Silverheels, Monty Hall and Alan Thicke.

■ Communist countries generally show little or no good (that is, American-style) TV programming. Even worse, most forbid commercials, causing serious bladder and urinary tract problems for their citizens.

■ While *some* freedom-loving Third World countries show reruns of old American sitcoms and westerns almost

exclusively, others brutally offer only domestic educational programs.

Interference with access to good Television is a human rights violation of the grossest kind. Strangely, though, both the United Nations and Amnesty International have remained silent about this. In your travels we suggest you boycott countries which do not allow their citizens continuous, quality viewing.

An Arabian Tuber watching black market tapes of I Love Lucy.

Foreign Phrases for the Couch Potato

Most foreign phrase books are useless if all you want to do is watch Television. Whether you are actually going abroad or merely viewing with your ethnic in-laws, you'll find these phrases useful.

English	Serbo-Croatian	Dutch	Italian	Finnish	German	French	Japanese
What's on TV?	Ša je na televiziji?	Wat is er op de TV?	Che fanno alla TV?	Mita teeveessä tulee?	Was ist am fernseher?	Qu'est ce qu'il y a la télé?	(Terebi Wa) nani yatteiru no?
While you're up, change the channel.	Dok stojiš, promijeni stanicu.	Als je toch opstaat, zet dan even een ander kanaal op.	A che ci sei, cambia canale.	Kun kerran olet ylhäällä, vaihda kanavaa.	Da du aufbist, schalte mal um.	Pendant que tu y es, change la chaine.	Tattasuide ni chaneru o kaete.
Out of my way! You make a better door than a window! (Or comparable phrase).	Molim te makni se! Nisi napravljen od stakla! ("You're not made of glass!")	Opzij! Je bent geschikter als deur dan als raam!	E spostati! Sai che hai delle belle spalle? ("Do you know you have beautiful shoulders?)"	Pois tieltä! En näe lävitsesi.	Mach' dass du aus meinem weg kommst, du bist doch nicht durchsichtig.	Pousse-toi d'la! Ton père n'était pas vitrier! ("Your father wasn't a glassmaker!")	Doite!
Please pass the beer.	Molim dodaj pivo!	Geef me het bier even aan.	Mi passi la birra, per favore?	Saisinko olutta.	Hol' mir bitte ein bier.	Passe moi une bière, s'il te plait.	Birru chodai.
Wait until the commercial.	Čekaj dok dodju reklame.	Kan het wachten tot de ster reklame?	Per piacere, aspetta sino al prossimo intervallo pubblicitano.	Odota mainoskatkoon saakka!	Warte bitte bis die reklamen gezeigt werden.	Attend jusqu'à la pub.	Kamasheru made matte.

Tuberland

One goal of the Couch Potato movement is Tuberland, the Couch Potato theme park project. Construction and realization of this park designed for Television enthusiasts will probably commence when the appropriate investors are found to finance the entire operation (any interested parties out there?).

Self-propelled mobile couches will be available to each visitor so that amusements may be enjoyed in a leisurely fashion.

PROPOSED PLAN INCLUDING HIGHLIGHTS OF

Tuberland

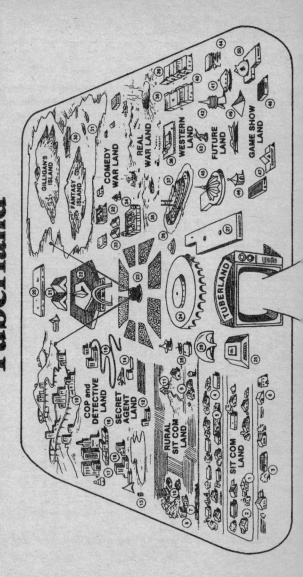

Tuberland

According to plan, Tuberland will be constructed near the Couch Potato World Headquarters in rural Dixon, California. Prime agricultural land has been selected as the appropriate site. Here, faithful replicas of rooms and buildings from time-honored TV programs will be interspersed with rides and amusements.

KEY TO MAP OF TUBERLAND

1. Cleaver Home
2. Nelson Residence
3. Partridge Family Rock/Disco Club
4. Arnold's *Happy Days* Drive-in Restaurant
5. Fred Sanford's Junkyard
6. Amos 'n Andy's Mystic Knights of the Sea Lodge Hall
7. Andy's Mayberry Courthouse
8. Shady Rest Hotel
9. *The Real McCoys* Farm
10. Arnold Ziffel Pig Pavilion
11. *Hee Haw* Mystery Outhouse
12. *Mission Impossible* Makeover Center
13. Maxwell Smart's Phone Booth
14. *Man/Girl From U.N.C.L.E.* Gadget Center
15. Car 54 Ride

16. *Kojak* Lollipop Shop
17. *Mod Squad* Boutique
18. Sgt. Friday's House of Facts
19. *Dukes of Hazzard/Streets of San Francisco* Car Chase Ride
20. Crazy House of Reception
21. Kiddie Show Center
22. Great Commercials of Western Man
23. Rabbit-Ear Plaza
24. Philo T. Farnsworth Viewerama
25. Soap Opera House
26. Chef Aldo's Video Kitchen
27. Television's Hall of Fame
28. TV Doghouse
29. Dr. Spudd's TV Guidance Center
30. *Loveboat* Computer Dating Service and Floating Restaurant
31. McHale's PT Boat Ride
32. *F Troop's* Fort Courage

33. Sgt. Bilko's Barracks
34. Stalag 13 Tunnel Ride
35. *Combat* Frontline Exhibit
36. *The Day After* Pavilion
37. *Maverick's* Lo-Ball Casino
38. Lusb La Rue's Discipline Ranch
39. Gunsmoked Barbeque Restaurant
40. Famous Saloons of the Old TV West
41. *My Favorite Martian* Spacecraft
42. *Star Trek* Beam-up Ride
43. Space Patrol Monument
44. Jetson Snax Drive-in
45. TV of Tomorrow Exhibit
46. *Queen for a Day* Coronation Room
47. *Wheel of Fortune* Finance Center
48. Tic Tac Dough Bakery
49. *The $25,000 Pyramid*
50. *Let's Make a Deal* Gift Emporium

For those who crave action-packed adventures, the Dukes of Hazzard/ Streets of San Francisco *car chase ride should prove to be exhilarating.*

The Crazy House of Reception will include, among its other zany attractions, a hall of giant TV screens where riders will be able to see themselves comically distorted though video interference.

The TV Doghouse, shown here next to the Ernie Kovaks Eternally-Lit-Cigar Memorial, will offer continuous showings of classic TV programs featuring famous canines like Rin-Tin-Tin, Lassie, Huckleberry Hound and Cleo the Basset Hound.

You'd be able to wheel your couch right up to the front lines and follow a look-alike of Combat's Sgt. Chip Saunders as he takes the old French farmhouse under heavy enemy fire in Real War Land.

Fast foods of tomorrow will be served up with quick-stop efficiency at the Judy Jetson Snack Bar in Futureland. A wide selection of foods specially developed by NASA to have uniform consistency will be offered to mobile couchers directly from the dispenser.

Encounter sessions with an audio-animatronic Mr. Ed will be available in Rural Sitcom Land.

AMERICAN TV POLL RESULTS —

☐ When asked, "Which medium would you give up if you had to?" only 8% said TV, compared with 22% for newspapers, 22% for radio and 49% for magazines.

☐ When asked to list the most important Black people in American history, respondents consistently rate the fictitious heroine Miss Jane Pittman highly. Said one: "Well, if she didn't exist, she should have."

☐ People were asked: "Not including your family, what do you consider the three most important things in your home?" Television topped the list, decisively beating out pets, beds, stoves and refrigerators.

☐ Heavy viewers of TV believe the outside world to be a much more dangerous place than light viewers. They also tend to be more moderate in their political views.

Couch Potatoes
and Politics

Many people erroneously think that the passive, accepting nature of Couch Potatoism precludes political involvement. While it is true that certain political practices—protest marches, for instance, or braving November's storms to vote—are beyond the tolerance of most Tubers, Couch Potatoes *are* keenly aware of current political events.

True, an avoidance impulse motivates much of this awareness. Elections, press conferences and other traumatic political events have a disconcertingly disruptive effect on regularly scheduled programming—it is no accident that videotape rentals go up every fourth November, as election coverage threatens to preempt everything worth watching. Smart Tubers stash away an emergency kit of cassettes for intrusive, unexpected world or domestic crises.

Despite an understandable tendency to avoid real life's interruptions of favorite TV fare, Tubers don't avoid *all* politics. On the contrary, when an issue touches our lives we can be spurred into action—of sorts.

Candidates and the
Couch Potatoes

Only unusually fervent stirrings of patriotic duty, mild November weather and a Sony Watchman can motivate a Couch Potato to attend the polls. To most Tubers this is a failing of the System: in a truly democratic society, we believe, one would be able to vote through one's two-way cable system (left).

Couch Potatoes' interest in politics usually transcends issues and positions. Instead Couch Potatoes, like most Americans, concentrate on the important things in a campaign: the quality of the candidates' commercials, how well the candidates come across on Television, whether we can stand to see their faces and hear their voices for an entire term of office.

Since we are so in tune with Television, we have been able to predict the last six elections with complete accuracy. Anybody could have seen that Eisenhower, a William Frawley look-alike riding *I Love Lucy*'s popularity, would beat Stevenson's *College Bowl* persona just by looking at the relative ratings of the two shows. Nixon lost to Kennedy in a time when handsome male leads were hot in shows like *My Three Sons* (Jack, Bobbie and Teddy?) and *Bachelor Father*, but he learned his lesson: in his next campaign, knowing he would never win on looks, he depended on comedy; his delivery of "Sock it to me?" on *Laugh-In* perfectly matched the mood of the viewing electorate. Reagan, previously a different kind of public servant as an actor on *GE Theatre*, clothed himself, his wife and most of his key appointees in the rich aura of *Dynasty* and *Dallas*.

In fact, it may be best in the future to forgo elections completely—just give each candidate his or her own show and see who does best in the Nielsen ratings.

Economic Programs

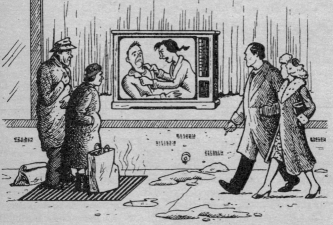

The need to view cuts across all social and economic boundaries.

Blatant self-interest colors the view of most Couch Potatoes. How we feel about welfare and government assistance seems to depend on how they affect us. We, like most people in our society, believe that hard work is ennobling—as long as somebody else does it.

In other words, less affluent Tubers, whose best years have been spent watching Andy Griffith reruns while on unemployment compensation, tend to favor a robust smorgasbord of government assistance with expanded benefits like HBO Stamps, Aid to TV-Dependent Children and the After-School Snacks Program. They tend to be Democrats.

Affluent Couch Potatoes, most of whom have inherited money and never had to work a day in their lives, speak with unique authority when they warn of the debilitating effects of slothfulness and undeserved money on the poor. They tend to be Republicans.

If you aren't sure where you stand in the spectrum, Couch Potato social scientists have developed the *Mighty Mouse* Political Litmus Test.

Political Litmus Test

Watch an episode of *Mighty Mouse* and note your reactions.

1. If you feel compelled to call congressional representatives in support of increasing Mighty Mouse's federal funding, you are a Democrat.

2. If you find yourself cheering for the cats, you are a Republican.

Couch Potatoes in War and Peace

Most Tubers are glad that the United States has finally gotten over the Vietnam syndrome— guilt and anguish over the Vietnam War (although a tiny but stubborn minority still argues that Vietnam was not a real place, just a long-running TV series that finally got canceled). Not that Couch Potatoes liked that or any war; it's just that we miss the military genre on TV, which all but disappeared in the wake of that unpopular war: shows like *Combat!*, *Gomer Pyle*, *Sgt. Bilko*, *McHale's Navy*, *M*A*S*H*, *Hogan's Heroes*, *Convoy*, *The Rat Patrol*, *Garrison's Gorillas* and *Baa Baa Black Sheep* as well as Cold War spy shows like *The Man From U.N.C.L.E.*, *The Avengers*, *I Spy*, *Secret Agent*, *Mission Impossible*, *I Led Three Lives* and *Get Smart*. Any fan of these can't help but be heartened by the fact that on Television war is becoming fun again.

Real-life war is another matter. Couch Potatoes are engaged in a relatively spirited debate over nuclear arms buildups and war.

Wally Buckley Pyne, president of Couch Potato Survivalists, Inc., represents one extreme. He says nuclear war offers a great opportunity for the Couch Potato Movement. "Most people would go berserk if they had to spend months on end in an enclosed room without sunshine, fresh air and outside distractions. For us Tubers, though, it would not be that different from everyday life."

Pyne claims his survivalists are well prepared to prevail after a nuclear holocaust, with underground lodges in remote areas stocked with generators, TVs, VCRs, toaster ovens and enough Twinkies, pizzas, Slim Jims, Good 'n Plenties, chips, Schlitz and videocassettes for several years—enough time, he believes, for food processors and TV networks to rise from the radioactive ashes.

"Since only a Tuber can thrive underground without rotting, we will be the seed potatoes of a whole new species, *Homo reclinus*," he claims. "This could be an evolutionary Great Lounge Forward."

Adlai Donahue of Tubers Against Nukes speaks for the other side. "Couch Potatoes do not want

A Couch Potato survivalist.

to risk being fried, steamed or baked," he says. "As the world cries out for better, affordable video equipment, our best technical resources and minds go for developing more devastating weapons." He states:

■ "Military spending in the United States is nearly $1,000 for every man, woman and Tater Tot *every year!* Think of the video components you could buy with that."

■ "For the cost of just six B-1 bombers, already obsolete when built, you could buy a video copy of *Debbie Does Dallas* for every heterosexual male west of Ogden, Utah."

In war, the first casualty could be Television. World War II froze the advancement of TV technology, and its bombs destroyed the only TV network in existence at the time. The next war would be worse, Donahue declares. The relatively few pieces of video equipment that survived a direct nuclear blast would be rendered useless by a potent surge of electromagnetic energy strong enough, reputable scientists believe, to burn out the electronic circuits of our TV sets, VCRs and automatic channel changers— even those protected in underground shelters.

And, tragically, the same electromagnetic pulse (EMP) would erase videotapes: "Yes, quite possibly *every* copy of *every* TV classic would be wiped out instantly and for eternity," says Donahue.

EMP: The ultimate Couch Potato fear

Appendix:
Couch Potato Lodges

This is a partial list of Couch Potato viewing lodges worldwide. If you wish to join a lodge in your area, or start your own, write to Couch Potato headquarters at P. O. Box 249, Dixon, CA 95620.

Couch Potato World Headquarters, Dixon, CA
Seeley's Seekers of Video Truth, Pasadena, CA
The 2010 Tele-Vista Chapter, Pasadena, CA
Iacino's Cathode Ray Tubers, Monrovia, CA
Sullivan's Brew 'n' View Chapter, Pasadena, CA
The House of Dandee Vision, Pasadena, CA
The Halladonian's Video Lair, Tuscaloosa, AL
The Princeton Principal Tubers, Princeton, WI
The Mobil Viewing Research Lodge, Worldwide
The Mystic Keepers of the Remote Control, Vallejo, CA - "Sit down and shut up."
Mr. Ned's Neighborhood, Los Angeles, CA - "Viewing is believing."
Philo T. Farnsworth Memorial Fraternity, Palo Alto, CA - "When the viewing gets weird, the weird get viewing."
South Mission Beach, San Diego, CA - "Watch till you drop."
The Single, Successful, Straight White Males, San Rafael, CA - "Today is the greatest day to drink ever."
The Visible Radio Society, North Hollywood, CA - "If they put it on TV, it must be good."
Tolos Multi-Screen Vacationland, Santa Monica, CA - "More sets, more shows."
The Eureka Sheiks, Eureka, CA - "What's on?"
The Neurological Order of Brewscaleros, Angels Camp, CA - "Don't tread on me."
The Church of the Subgenius, Dallas, TX - "Too much is always better than not enough."
The Hillcrest Manor Video Guild, State College, PA - "TV party tonight!"
The Lounge Rangers, Whittier, CA - "Fried spuds and suds and our TV, we cherish more than activity."
The Legion of Video Vegetables, Greenwich Village, NY - "Shoot the cat, he's blocking the TV."
Comics and Comix, Berkeley, CA - "There is no television but television turned on."
The Channing University Alumni Association, Barboursville, WV - "There is no death, only syndication."
The Mar Vista Grounded Grid, Los Angeles, CA
The Bloomington Couch Potatoes, Bloomington, IN
The Twonkie Zone, St. Louis, MO - "Deut mon Dei."
The Pittsburgh Potatoes for Boob Tube Viewing, Pittsburgh, PA - "We regret we have only 24 hours a day to give to our boob-tubing."
The Grand Yam's Michigan Chapter, West Bloomfield, MI
The Ben Lomond TV Warriors, Ben Lomond, CA
American Precision Viewers, Redwood City, CA - "Brewski! Brewski!"
The North Coast East Chapter of the Loyal Order of Couch Potatoes, Cleveland, OH
The Vegetable Oysters, Lafayette, IN - "We'd sell members of our immediate family if they interrupted our viewing."
The Theodore Bilbo Memorial Chapter, Portland, OR - "Keeping our airwaves smut-free."
The Frito Layabouts, Menlo Park, CA - "E Pluribus Starch - Cogito Ergo Alcohol."
The Larrabee Lounge Lizards, West Hollywood, CA

The Spuds of the Sod, San Francisco, CA - Translated from Gaelic: "Thanks be to God for strong beer and smashed potatoes."

The Church of the Immaculate '60 Chevy, Sacramento, CA

The Nest, Davis, CA - "You make a better door than a window."

The Channel Hoppers, Louisville, KY

The No. 1 San Jose Pringle Contingent, San Jose, CA - "The potato in the ground grows, the potato out of ground rots."

The Masses, Fulton, MD - "One person, one channel."

Prime New Mexico, Albuquerque, NM - "You are what you watch."

Oasis Acres, Citrus Heights, CA - "Do it later."

The All-Seeing Tubers, Albuquerque, NM - "TV Tuber Alles."

The Doylestown Tubers, Doylestown, PA - "Watch free or die."

The First Far Eastern Chapter, Kobe, Japan

Club de Canadien Couch Potato, Kitchener, Ontario, Canada - "Viva le Beave."

The M. Dower's Home, Seattle, WA - "A good TV is a good friend."

The Slug Saloon, Monterey, CA - "I'll do it during the commercial."

The Sunset Tubers, San Francisco, CA - "Born to view."

The Cysters of Tubal Libation, Berkeley, CA - "Tomatoes Abondanza."

The Faculty Lounge and Unhealth Spa-Foon, Shawnee Mission, KS - "Memento mori, memento meri, memento Curly, Moe & Larry."

Mel's Tender Tuners, Los Angeles, CA - "Do they deliver?"

The Comment Taters, New York, NY - "To think is human, to view, divine."

Jose Feliciano School of Visual Arts - "Shoot 'em in the back."

The Bluelight House for the Reclined, Rohnert Park, CA - "We've got a nose for TV."

Gallagher's Bar and Grill, Santa Barbara, CA - "Sit 'n' view with your favorite brew."

The Smashed Potatoes, Monterey, CA

The West Hills Wastrels, Portland, OR - "Thank GOD for cable."

The Spudniks - Cosmo's Casbah, Roanoke, VA - "Better to have viewed in vain, than never to have viewed at all."

The Mighty Cathodians, Keepers of the Tube, Glassboro, NJ - "Hey, let's put on a show."

The Terrapins for Trivia, College Park, MD - "We are *all* potatoes under the skin."

The Barker Hotel, Vancouver, BC - "There is no greater star than Don Knotts."

The Tubular Belles, Lebanon, NH - "Vita in tubus vitreus" (Life in a glass tube).

The Bosom Buddies, Exton, PA - "Suffering Succotash!"

Woofy's Looney Tuners, Salem, OR - "Sofa, so good!"

Danny's Deviant Dial Twisters, San Jose, CA

National Association of Staring Americans (NASA), St. Charles, IL - "Live to watch, watch to live."

Spudburbia Sofa Setters, Williamsville, NY - "The eyes have it."

The Family, Nashville, TN - "*Anybody* can watch the good shows."

Delta Koppa High (Δ KH), Schaumburg, IL - "The fries, they be stickin' together."

Virginia Creature Watchers, Arlington, VA - "Never pass up a monster movie."

Reality's Refugees, Houston, TX - "Mind alteration while U wait."

Richmond Rerun Rangers, Richmond, VA - "Run the channels."

The Alpha Epsilon Fraternity of Viewers (Σ AE), Berkeley, CA - "Ore-Ida!"

The Melrose-Avers Viewing Society, Chicago, IL - "Vini, Vidi, Trinitron."

The Cathode Ray Mission, San Francisco, CA - "The television screen has become the retina of the mind's eye."

Cosmic Ennui, Fairbanks, AK - "Never call us during *Hill St. Blues.*"

The Video Artists Clubhouse, South Bend, IN - "Be it raster or be it vector - keep it 4 × 3."

Karks, San Anselmo, CA - "Only view.".

The Doctor Doom-TV-Tub-Rabbit-Ear Club, Martinez, CA - "Sleep tight tonight your air force is awake."

The Tahoe Tubers, Salinas, CA - "Slope spuds on skis."

Talismanic, Misawa, Japan - "Fitness through food."

The Video Fleurnies, New York, NY - "What time is 9:30?"

The Cave, Knoxville, TN - "Turn on, tune in, veg out."

Waveriders, Honolulu, HI - "Locked into the tube."

Rocking Spud Ranch, Tucson, AZ - "Where the beer and the rabbit ears play."

The Mystic Krewe of View, Charlotte, NC - "I like Ike, but I love Lucy."

Video Taters, Baltimore, MD - "We shall view until the golden gong of the universe beckons."

Mountain Tubers, Montgomery Center, VT - "Winter is tube time—especially mud season."

The Beautiful Downtown Russet Burbank Chapter, St. Louis, MO - "Turn it up a little."

The Cot-tage Couchers, Mt. Clemens, MI - "All eyes forward."

The Finegan Palace, South Lebannon, OH

The United Office Potatoes of Southern Wisconsin, Janesville, WI

The Hypnotized Hoard, Jacobus, PA

Pommes de Terres, Boise, ID - "We're appealing."

Couch Sexpots, Rolling Hills Estates, CA - "TV turns us on."

Royal Order of the Water Buffalo, Richmond, CA - "Maynard G. Krebbs is the new messiah."

Niemiec Nuzzlers, Scottsdale, AZ - "We'll never roam cuz we stay at home, we're Couch Potatoes, rah, rah, rah."

Jack Webb Fundamental Lodge #127, Lyman, WA - "Just the facts, ma'am."

The Potato Mashers, Inkster, MI

The Ancient and Honorable Order of the Old Panasonic, San Francisco, CA - "What else is on?"

Society of Potatoes United to Develop Stagnation (S.P.U.D.S.), Lansing, MI

The Greater Boston Visionary Outpost, Allston, MA - "Beer, Whiskey and Cable."

The Kouch Katahdins, Coldwater, MI - "We're the STP team: spuds are terrific people."

The French Fried Potatoes, Pacific Grove, CA - "Toujours Trinitron."

The Potomac Tubers, Arlington, VA - "Holding Horizontally."

The Fred Mertz Foundation for Creative Obesity, Palo Alto, CA - "Ritz, schlitz, and bacon bits; never mind the ugly zits."

The Order of Vegetables, Baltimore, MD - "Couch Potatoes—the final frontier."

The M*A*S*H Potatoes, Phoenix, AZ - "Suds for spuds."

The Snag City Red Eyes, Dillingham, AK - "Give me TV or give me head."

Tuber or Not Tuber Lodge, Norwood, MA - "Reclino ergo sum."

Spongers, Tarpon Springs, FL - "In sponging there is truth."

The Vic Morrow Memorial Lodge, Brooklyn, NY - "Black and white power!"

The Tubular Bells, San Rafael, CA - "Come on, big bucks, big bucks!"

Pajaro Dunes Fire Dept., Watsonville, CA - "It's nappy time!"

The Lumpy Lake Park Gazers, Hinckley, OH - "If you got it, watch it!"

The Mystic Knights of the See, Oklahoma City, OK - "Out to lunch with Ho Ho."

The Curly, Larry and Moe Memorial Lodge, Hamilton, Ontario - "Nyuk, nyuk, nyuk, toin up the volume."

The Raster Pasture, Vancouver, BC - "Gaze'n and Graze'n."

Real Food, Bloomfield, NJ - "Reality enables all life for order or death."

The Catatonic Couch Potatoes, Bolinas, CA - "Semper Televisus et Felis!"

The Sportaholics, Falls Church, VA - "This spud's for you."

Bob's Boob Tubes, Eastlake, OH - "A Couch Potato is a proud potato."

The A and B Group, Haledon, NJ - "It's better to do it with a friend."

The Venetian Viewers, Venice, CA - "We like to watch."

The Granada Video Invaders, London, England - "Not all British TV is bad!"

The Spud Ranch, Berkeley, CA - "Oh give us a home where the Trinitrons roam."